"*Finding Your Way* by Gary \[a life complete in serving and ⌐.....ing jesus Christ. It is a life filled with awe, hope, and expectation for a better way of living each day as he has so clearly written. I would recommend it as a reading for everyone."

Gordon E. Heffern, Retired Chairman and CEO,
Society Corporation, Cleveland, Ohio

"So frequently, Christians struggle in today's fast-paced society with the question, 'How can I know I am in the center of God's will?' Gary has done a wonderful job answering this question using biblical truth confirmed with a multitude of relevant, real-life examples. This is a 'tool' we can all use to come closer to understanding and following God's will for our lives."

Don Mitchell, Chairman of the Board, CBMC International

"Gary has created a brilliant 'Handbook for Living' that will help you get the most out of your life. Regardless of your circumstances, the insightful, profound truths in this book will point you in the right direction and lead you on the path toward your true destiny. It is the perfect Guidebook for leading a productive, fulfilled life!"

Tom Brooks, Creative Director, Worship Alliance

"In *Finding Your Way*, Gary LaFerla draws upon his years as a pastor and businessman and handles tough questions with wisdom and encouragement. Richly illustrated and biblically grounded, his book offers real guidance for those who long for direction and meaning."

Ravi Zacharias, speaker and author of *The Real Face of Atheism*

"Gary brings a refreshingly uncomplicated perspective to those questions faced by men and women alike. Is there an intersection of God's will, and my want? Is it right to inquire of the Almighty? And to desire an answer? Let Gary hold your hand as together you search the unsearchable truth of God's Will."

Sean McConlogue
President of Affinity Insurance Services, LLC

"*The* playbook for understanding what it means to walk with Christ."

Jim Ryun, congressman, three-time Olympian

To: Lucy & Martin May God Bless You!

finding your way

A Guide to Discovering God's Best for Your Life

Gary LaFerla

BakerBooks

Grand Rapids, Michigan

Published by Baker Books
a division of Baker Publishing Group
P.O. Box 6287, Grand Rapids, MI 49516-6287
www.bakerbooks.com

Printed in the United States of America

Library of Congress Cataloging-in-Publication Data
LaFerla, Gary.
     Finding your way : a guide to discovering God's best for your life / Gary LaFerla.
          p.   cm.
     Includes bibliographical references.
     ISBN 0-8010-6530-5 (pbk.)
     1. Vocation—Christianity. 2. Christian life. 3. God—Will. 4. Providence and government of God. I. Title.
BV4740.L34 2005
248.4—dc22   2004022634

Unless otherwise indicated, Scripture is taken from the New King James Version. Copyright © 1982 by Thomas Nelson, Inc. Used by permission. All rights reserved.

Scripture marked KJV is taken from the King James Version of the Bible.

Scripture marked TLB is taken from *The Living Bible*, copyright © 1971. Used by permission of Tyndale House Publishers, Inc., Wheaton, Illinois 60189. All rights reserved.

Scripture marked NASB is taken from the New American Standard Bible®, Copyright © 1960, 1962, 1963, 1968, 1971, 1972, 1973, 1975, 1977, 1995 by The Lockman Foundation. Used by permission.

Scripture marked NCV is taken from the New Century Version®. Copyright © 1987, 1988, 1991 by Word Publishing, a division of Thomas Nelson, Inc. Used by permission. All rights reserved.

Scripture marked NIV is taken from the HOLY BIBLE, NEW INTERNATIONAL VERSION®. NIV®. Copyright © 1973, 1978, 1984 by International Bible Society. Used by permission of Zondervan. All rights reserved.

Scripture marked NLT is taken from the *Holy Bible*, New Living Translation, copyright © 1996. Used by permission of Tyndale House Publishers, Inc., Wheaton, Illinois 60189. All rights reserved.

Scripture marked Phillips is taken from The New Testament in Modern English, revised edition—J. B. Phillips, translator. © J. B. Phillips 1958, 1960, 1972. Used by permission of Macmillan Publishing Co., Inc.

To

Debbie, Chelsea, and Christopher

Contents

Foreword

I HAVE TRAVELED extensively throughout the world and have met people of all ages and nationalities. As I listen to personal, and often gripping, stories of individuals, one thing becomes very clear—the decisions that people make impact their lives forever. Wouldn't it be nice to make wise choices and decisions all of the time!? Wouldn't it be nice to *know* what God wants you to do in any given situation?

Gary LaFerla addresses the important issue of knowing God's will for your life by taking a look at key issues that help us make godly choices and decisions on a daily basis.

As an evangelist and Christian leader, I have seen the effects that poor decision making and ungodly choices have had on people's lives. I have seen highly successful leaders fail and come up empty because of poor decision making. I have also met many struggling individuals who are experiencing the scars of divorce, sexual promiscuity, addiction, and other tragedies. If people made wise choices, they could avoid some very hurtful and difficult situations in life.

Making wise decisions and godly choices, however, is not limited to moral issues. Sometimes the hardest choices

9

(for example, in careers, education, marriage, or finance) are those that don't appear to be good or bad. Yet making the wrong choice in any one of these areas of life can lead to an unfulfilled and unhappy state of being! No matter what kind of choice or decision you need to make, knowing what God wants you to do is vital. He has a divine purpose for your life and wants to be involved in every detail of your day-to-day living.

This book will help guide you through the maze of difficult choices you face and clearly show you that God is at work in your life. I've seen clear evidence of God at work in my own life since I made the choice to trust God's Son, Jesus Christ, at a Christian camp when I was twelve years old. That wise choice has made an impact on my life and helped steer me in the right direction. Since that day as a twelve year old, however, I have had to make countless decisions and choices in my life. I can't imagine how different my life would have been if I had made those decisions without God's help.

You are about to embark on an important journey. In the following pages you will learn how to discover God's will for your life on a very practical day-to-day basis. Take the time to read and digest Gary LaFerla's words of wisdom. Each chapter is rich, meaningful, and personal—in fact, you will feel like you are being personally mentored.

Gary LaFerla's extensive experience working with people as both a business consultant and pastor has given him a solid background to help you in your decision-making process. In his work with international business, crusade evangelism, and ministry, he has successfully counseled individuals, business leaders, and companies. As you discover the tools to make right decisions, and the joy of knowing God's will, you will be on the path to a fulfilled and joyous life.

Luis Palau

Preface

HAVE YOU DESIRED an exciting and fulfilling life that touches others in significant ways and leaves a lasting heritage for generations to come? What if I told you that God has intended your life to be a great adventure, better than any action film or classic drama that you have enjoyed watching on movie screens? My goal is that you *find your way* to the life that God wants you to live and that you experience it to the fullest.

When I first set out to write this book, my intention was to simply reach the world with the greatest news of human history—the gospel of Jesus Christ! I want people everywhere to know about the incredible *power* that is available for them when they unlock the door of God's destiny for their lives. I also want people to experience the awesome *peace* that is available to them by knowing Christ and His love! Finally, I want people to realize God's fantastic *plan* for their lives, a plan that is beyond their wildest dreams or personal desires.

God does have an awesome plan for your life. In fact He calls out to us in many ways each day, desiring to bring us into a closer relationship with Him. He does so through our experience of His creation, His divine providence, His Word, the intervention of His Son, Jesus Christ, in human history, and in other ways. The purpose of this book is to point you to God and open your spiritual eyes, ears, and heart to Him so that you can understand and follow His great plan for your life.

Following the Creator's plan is a lot like following the manufacturer's instructions that come with most products you buy. I can't count how many times during the Christmas season I have bought toys for my children and thrown the instructions aside as I said to my wife, "Of course I know how to put this thing together." Typically I would break some important piece trying to force it to fit, and of course there was always some little part left over when I was finished building—a part that I would find out was vital to the proper operation of the toy! After it was done and the toy didn't work, I would be forced to follow the instructions and put the toy together all over again the right way. Naturally this took at least twice the amount of time than it would have taken had I just followed the directions my first time through.

Often today people live their lives just like my toy story at Christmas. They rush through life, in a hurry to get to some great ending point, putting all the parts of life together quickly with little consideration and direction. They move through the normal phases of life, including schools, careers, marriage(s), kids, and vacations with good intentions and the goal of trying to enjoy life as much as possible. Often, however, years pass by without even the slightest consideration of what God may have desired for them. Then one day they wake up and sadly realize that much of their life has passed them by. The results are often the same: little time with the ones they loved most, unfulfilled dreams, high stress, and sometimes the shattered lives of significant people they have loved. Looking back into their past, we might find that they have forced little "parts" into their lives that didn't fit and left out the most important "part," which is God and His guidance.

Other people may know about God and even have a relationship with Him but do not have a solid understanding about God's will and His principles of guidance for life. After failing to consult God's instruction manual and making decisions that fail, they say something like, Why did God let this happen to me? And there are other people who are curious about God and want to know about His will and how it might impact them. Perhaps one of these examples describes your own life.

No matter what your experience in life has been, I have some great news for you. Life doesn't have to be dull, unfulfilling, disappointing, or a series of broken dreams or unfulfilled desires. God has the master instruction plan for your life and is calling you to consult it. He welcomes you to a deep relationship with Him and has the power to make all things new again. No matter what stage of life you may be in now, from your teens to your nineties, God can change things. It is never too late to find your way with God. How incredible life can be when we connect with God and begin to realize the wonderful purposes and plans that He has individually designed for each of us!

I encourage you to get alone and take time to read this book carefully with pen and paper in hand. Pray before you read, jotting down your dreams, desires, and goals. Consider what God's will may be for your life and the reasons why you may have held back from pursuing it. Note your fears and hesitations. Discuss these with a person whom you trust, and then begin to launch out in faith.

My prayer for you as you read this book is that your eyes will be opened to the wonderful and divine will of God as it is found in His Word, the Bible, God's master instruction manual for our lives. I pray that you will be challenged to live the great adventure that only He can grant for you to live.

Remember, the greatest achievement that any person can attain is to know God and enjoy life in and through His will. This book was written to help you get there! God bless you in your search for His destiny and remember that He has a plan and will accomplish it, if you will let Him!

May you find God's best and experience the great adventure that He has for you as you find your way in Him!

Acknowledgments

I WOULD LIKE to express my deep gratitude to the following people who worked so tirelessly to help make this book a reality: Melinda Kay Ronn, my agent, editor, and publicist; Creston Mapes, my creative editor; Bill Petersen and everyone at Baker Books, who have so wonderfully brought this book into being; my in-house staff—Cathy Snyder, Kathy Shipman, Corrine Pavkov, and Desi Becker—who spent endless hours proofreading, copying and working to meet deadlines; our reading team, including Wendy Eller, Anne Marie Segedy, Cathy Miller, Lynn Herman, Ann Huntley, Karen Wayman, Pat Blubaugh, and Pamela Courrier; and Sonia Blake, who took the initiative to help get this book off the ground with her invaluable transcription work.

My heartfelt thanks to Luis Palau for his wise counsel and time and to his son Kevin for his friendship and his vision; to everyone at Calvary Chapel of Akron for diligently praying and supporting this book; to my wonderful wife,

Debbie, and our children, Chelsea and Christopher, for their constant inspiration and support each day.

Finally and most important, I thank God for making everything possible in His time. He has granted us eternal life through His Son and sent His Spirit to guide us to glory.

1

God's Calling

Purposeful Living

On October 31, 1983, Korean Airlines flight 007 departed from Anchorage, Alaska, for a direct flight to Seoul, Korea. Unknown to the crew, however, the computer engaging the flight navigation system contained a one-and-a-half-degree routing error. At the point of departure, the mistake was unnoticeable. One hundred miles out, the deviation was still so small as to be undetectable. But as the giant 747 continued through the Aleutians and out over the Pacific, the plane strayed increasingly from its proper course. Eventually it was flying over Soviet airspace.

Soviet radar picked up the error, and fighter jets scrambled into the air to intercept. Over mainland Russia the jets shot flight 007 out of the sky, and all aboard lost their lives.[1]

The choices we make in life will greatly alter our destiny. God is reaching out from heaven to you today and offering His divine wisdom to guide your life to success and fulfillment. He has navigational directions and a life course all set—just for you! The choice to accept His direction is yours.

Call to Me, and I will answer you, and show you great and mighty things, which you do not know.

Jeremiah 33:3

IF YOU ARE LIKE most people, you have found yourself in a situation more than once when you've cried out, "Speak to me, God. Email me. Fax me. But tell me what I should do here!"

Are you searching for answers to life's problems? Do you want to discover the true purpose for your existence? Take comfort! God wants to direct you. His desire is that all people understand His will. The sad truth, however, is that most people die before ever knowing God deeply and experiencing the wonderful blessings He has in store for them.

Many go through life with a lack of purpose, lamenting their situation, wishing they had direction, craving a life of meaning. Some look back on their lives with deep sorrow, regretting the day they made a fateful mistake. Others lie awake at night wondering where they went wrong, wishing they had a chance to do things differently. And still others—maybe you—are buried beneath problems that seem too monumental to overcome.

One thing is certain—when you look to God for help and direction, you are not seeking a way out of your human responsibility or an excuse for hidden fears. No. When you seek God's help, that is wisdom! That is faith! It is the cry of

18

a man or woman who really wants to excel in life, who wants to understand, who wants to make the right choices.

God's Wisdom

Many people want to believe there is someone who cares about them and who wants to guide them. Today let it be known that there is a God who speaks, and He is the God of love. He wants to show you how to hear from Him, how to let Him guide you, and how to rest in His abounding love.

Recently I was listening to a radio interview with some financial analysts. A caller asked one of the analysts if it was prudent to pray about selecting a particular stock as an investment. There was some laughing and joking, of course, but when the analyst answered the question, I was taken aback. He said, "Yes, it is prudent to pray about your selection of stocks. God is interested in your financial welfare and your overall life. The Bible speaks about salvation but also about many other areas of life, including finances."

This is an incredible insight into Scripture. Practically speaking, God wants you to seek Him regarding all the major decisions you need to make in life. He wants your decision-making process to be guided by His wisdom. Whether you need to make a decision regarding financial investments, a major purchase, a career change or job promotion, education, vacations, medical care, or a lifetime mate in marriage, God wants you to seek His guidance to ensure that you make the right decision.

The Lord cares about all of your needs—small and great. Be encouraged! It is not God's character to hide His will from you. Contrary to many people's understanding, God does not desire to play "hide-and-seek" or "catch Me if you can" with your life's destiny. Instead, He has a very specific will and plan for your life, and He longs to reveal it to you. Isn't that awesome?

When you get to know God personally, you will learn not to worry about life's problems, circumstances, and predicaments. Instead, you will bring each of your needs and cares to Him and watch Him work.

Isn't it tragic that, even though we live in a society in which knowledge of God and His Word is readily available, we still fail to understand—even reject—His counsel? As a result the decisions we make generate much anxiety, frustration, anger, and hardship. Yet all the while, God is right there in our presence wanting to help us and guide us for His glory. Yes, there will be times of silence from heaven, but let me assure you that even in silence you will find a sure form of guidance as you learn to wait on God in faith.

How does God answer? How does He intervene on your behalf to guide and direct your path? F. B. Meyer, the great British pastor who lived from 1847 to 1929, commented: "Before taking a partner in life, entering into business with another, or yielding assent to any proposition which involves a confederation with others—be sure to ask counsel at the mouth of the Lord. He will assuredly answer by an irresistible impulse; by the voice of a friend; by a circumstance strange and unexpected; by a passage of scripture. He will choose his own messenger; but he will send a message."[2]

God's very nature shows His ability to guide you. He is omnipotent (all-powerful), omniscient (all-knowing), and omnipresent (present in all places at all times).

God is able. He is there for you and can guide you through every struggle, battle, sorrow, temptation, need, and question. He can do anything.

Many people believe God is not in the business of directing their daily affairs. Instead, they put Him in a box, believing His sole purpose is to lead people to salvation (eternal life) and then leave them to fend for themselves. Fortunately, this is the opposite of the truth.

God's will for your life is all-encompassing. The Scriptures clearly show that His will for you includes salvation, purpose, and abundant life! Psalm 37:23 says: "The steps of the godly are directed by the LORD. He delights in every detail of their lives" (NLT).

God's General Will

God's design for you is to bring you to Christ and mold you into the image of His Son. He wants your character to resemble that of Jesus so you will share His love for people and bring glory to Him through your life. "The Lord is not slow in doing what he promised—the way some people understand slowness. But God is being patient with you. He does not want anyone to be lost, but he wants all people to change their hearts and lives" (2 Pet. 3:9 NCV). This work of God will continue until the end of the age. We are moving quickly toward this time that is described in the Bible as a time of judgment, after which the kingdom of God will be established on the earth.

Salvation is more than just a commitment or prayer. Salvation is the ultimate life experience. Through salvation you get to know the Creator personally and enjoy His true fulfillment. When you accept Christ as your Savior, you soon learn that there is a much more important aspect of life than what you see in the physical realm. The veil to the unseen world rushes open and a new and refreshing spiritual side of life is revealed. Only through the experience of salvation can we come to know the truth about life, creation, and the kingdom of God. It is, therefore, the most important aspect of life. It releases you from the weight of destructive sin and enables you to know the very One who created you. It's true—the fulfilling life you seek is found only in the fountain of life, Jesus Christ.

God's Particular Will

Everything we need to understand God's general will (salvation) is found directly in the Scriptures. However, when we come to God's particular will, the information in the Bible is not always so clear-cut. Decisions about relationships, the purchase of a home, relocation, or a career choice are major and life changing. When you face decisions such as these, you need God's guidance; however, in the past you may have found it difficult to discern that guidance.[3]

Many Bible scholars have made this statement concerning the will of God: "Ninety percent of God's will for your life is found in the Bible." This is true, but people often respond by saying, "It's the other 10 percent that really frustrates me."

Are you struggling with a decision you need to make? Are you wondering what God wants you to do? Be encouraged! God desires to help you. He has given you guidelines to know His particular will. He cares about the details of your life, and He won't fail to make His will known if you truly seek His guidance.

Jesus stressed this fact when He said, "Two sparrows cost only a penny, but not even one of them can die without your Father's knowing it. God even knows how many hairs are on your head. So don't be afraid. You are worth much more than many sparrows" (Matt. 10:29–31 NCV).

The Bible offers several keys to knowing God's will for your life and to help you make God-centered decisions that will transform you and the lives of others. Bear in mind that these keys may not answer every question or need in your life. But they will make your life's path smoother and easier to travel while giving you the confidence to make wise choices, which will lead to a rewarding life.

The more knowledge you have regarding God's will, and the greater your understanding of His Word, the more you will experience His blessed guidance. Ephesians 5:17 says: "Don't act thoughtlessly, but try to understand what the Lord wants you to do" (NLT).

Everyone's concerns are different. The decisions you consider vitally important may not be the concerns of others, because God did not make the human race like Ford makes Mustangs or like Mrs. Fields makes cookies— cookie-cutter copies. You are being individually crafted, molded, and shaped into His image. He has given you a one-of-a-kind personality, individual desires, a unique emotional makeup, particular physical traits, and special talents and gifts. God's will for each one of us is unique. God has given each of us a calling—a particular purpose in life. When you realize that calling, you will begin to understand His will for you.

God's Call

According to Scripture, God calls each person to a life of purpose and blessing for His glory (see Gen. 1:27–28; Eph. 2:10). Blessing without purpose is unfulfilling personally and unproductive for God's kingdom. But when you begin to realize God's purpose for your life, then you will begin to enjoy a meaningful existence, as life becomes all God planned it to be.

In essence, the calling of God is a specific purpose for which He created you. This calling normally becomes realized after you come to salvation in Christ. It is then that the lights start turning on and you become better and better acquainted with the Lord and begin to understand the grand purposes He has for you.

The "ultimate life experience," the "highest good," the "greatest life ever lived" can describe the lives of people who have fulfilled the call of God. Indeed, the call of God answers the ultimate "Why?" of our existence: Why was I created? What is my purpose in life?

Many Christians think *God's call* refers only to religious service in professional ministry as pastors, missionaries, or members of the clergy. Unfortunately, this wrong distinction has left millions of believers in the dark regarding God's will for their lives. If you do not come to an understanding of God's purpose and guidance for your life, you will cheat yourself out of the ultimate blessing of knowing the reason for your existence.

To prepare you for His call, God gives you gifts, which include particular talents and abilities that He wants you to use to glorify Him. Have you ever noticed that some people are born communicators? When they speak, you listen. Their teaching skills are obvious. They are easily understood and what they teach is accepted. Others are born artists. You can drop virtually any common thing into their hands and they can make it into a work of art. Then there are those who are gifted administrators, people who are able to make order out of chaos—and enjoy the process!

Some people are gifted with leadership skills, able to march a group of people over hurdles, around obstacles, and directly to a planned objective or goal. Still others are born musicians and can create and perform all sorts of melodies that for others would be impossible. Some people are technically orientated and have a great love for scientific data. They derive pleasure using their brainpower to bring great innovations into our lives.

The point is that God wants to use *your* particular gifts and dreams to bring Him glory and to fulfill your life in a most spectacular way. Similarly, He gives you *spiritual gifts* so you can communicate the truths of Christ to the world, as well as build up His church. These gifts are listed in Scripture.

Reading them can make for an eye-opening and worthwhile investment of your time (see Rom. 12:6–8; 1 Cor. 12:4–31; Eph. 4:11–12). Remember that spiritual giftedness and innate talent—talent you are born with—may be different, and yet they can work hand in hand for the glory of God.

For example, consider how the world would be a different place had not a few individuals sensed God's call in their lives and used their God-given talents. Where would we be if R. G. LeTourneau had never created the giant earth-moving machines that carved America's roadways or if J. C. Penney had never pioneered retail sales in America? What if missionary Hudson Taylor had never brought Christ and a new way of life to China, reformers like William Wilber-force had not brought an end to slavery, and politicians like Abraham Lincoln had never changed the face of America? The list goes on, from Olympic gold medal winner Eric Liddell to NASCAR champion Jeff Gordon, from inventor George Washington Carver to philosopher and defender of the Christian faith Francis Schaeffer.

In this book I will tell the stories of many people who have realized their call in life. These stories will describe many different lives, from the most common to the most elite. Those who have made an impact in this world and enjoyed abundant life in Christ have consistently had two things in common:

1. They knew Christ.
2. They had a desire to follow His call for their lives.

Perhaps you have had the desire to seek God's will for your life but have found yourself saying, *What will I be commit-ting myself to doing?* Perhaps visions of being a missionary in Africa pop into your mind. Or you may think, *Why should I seek God when I can manage on my own?*

You may have had difficult life experiences that deter you from even considering the idea of doing God's will.

Realize this: God has a custom-designed plan for *your* life. No matter what situation you are in today, He desires to use you as a blessed instrument for His divine glory.

God's Blueprint for Life

God has your life well in control. Jeremiah 1:4–5 says: "Before I made you in your mother's womb, I chose you. Before you were born, I set you apart for a special work. I appointed you as a prophet to the nations" (NCV). These beautiful words were spoken not only for Jeremiah's benefit but for ours. God has designed you for a purpose. He has given you specific desires and dreams and set you apart for a special work. You were created with certain innate abilities and gifts—for a specific reason. As with Jeremiah, God has an express interest in your life.

In Psalm 139:15–16 we read: "You were there while I was being formed in utter seclusion! You saw me before I was born and scheduled each day of my life before I began to breathe. Every day was recorded in your Book" (TLB). Did you catch that? God has every day of your life scheduled! Nothing happens in your life by accident. He has a divine plan and purpose for you and wants you to understand what it is. By identifying the gifts, abilities, and desires He has given you and by surrendering your life to Him, you will have a fuller understanding of His call.

As the following chapters help you unlock the keys to knowing the will of God, you will begin to see God's blueprint for your life. The soul mate you desire in marriage, the family you presently have, the career, the dream, the crisis you find yourself in, and, yes, even your very smallest decisions in life can all be brought to God for His guidance.

I sincerely pray that you will come to understand as you read this book that you have been created for a purpose. When this truth penetrates your heart, may you step confidently toward God and take hold of His call for your life. This is what Esther did when she realized God had something special for her to do. "What's more, who can say but that you have been elevated to the palace for just such a time as this?" (Esther 4:14 NLT). Here is Esther's story:

Queen Vashti, the queen of Persia, performed an act of incredible arrogance against the king. She refused to honor a special invitation to come to his court. The king's court punished her by removing her as queen. A search was made throughout the empire for her replacement.

By the providential hand of God, a young Jew named Esther was chosen to succeed Queen Vashti as the new queen of Persia. Esther, who had great beauty and poise, came from a humble background. At the time, she certainly could have had no idea about the incredible purpose God had for her life in the days ahead.

Haman, an enemy of the Jews in Persia, had a master plan to exterminate all the Jews from the kingdom. Mordecai, Esther's uncle, unveiled the plan to Esther and told her that as the new queen she must act immediately and reveal the plot to the king. Time was of the essence, as the lives of thousands of innocent men, women, and children hung in the balance. Esther did not know that because of the divine hand of God, the destiny of the Jews lay in her hands. God was calling her!

Mordecai sent a message to Esther revealing Haman's evil plot and the written decree to destroy all the Jews. Mordecai begged Esther to intercede for her people. Esther sent word back to Mordecai, saying, "The whole world knows that anyone who appears before the king in his inner court without being invited is doomed to die unless the king holds out his gold scepter. And the king has not called for me to come to him in more than a month" (4:11 NLT).

Esther was fearful. At first, she was not clear about God's calling. However, Mordecai sent another urgent message to her. He said, "Don't think for a moment that you will escape there in the palace when all other Jews are killed. If you keep quiet at a time like this, deliverance for the Jews will arise from some other place, but you and your relatives will die. What's more, who can say but that you have been elevated to the palace for just such a time as this?" (vv. 13–14 NLT).

Esther petitioned the king and revealed Haman's evil plot. As a result, the king had Haman put to death and a new decree was issued protecting the Jews throughout Persia. Once Esther understood God's call on her life, He used her in a magnificent way and she experienced a life of great blessing.

God has great things for your life as He did for Esther's life. But His plan may not be clear just yet. He has much in store for you, but you must take the first step to knowing His will by saying, "I will follow You wherever You lead!" That is precisely what William Wilberforce did.

When the Englishman Wilberforce sought counsel about determining God's will for his life from close friend John Newton, a prominent slave trader turned Christian who later wrote the classic hymn "Amazing Grace," Newton advised Wilberforce against going into ministry.

"You need to spend your life doing one thing," said Newton, "the thing God has called you to do and that you feel in your heart is necessary." That "one thing," for Wilberforce, was bringing an end to slavery.

Historians say Wilberforce wasn't cut out for such a daunting task. He didn't excel in parliament. He wasn't exactly a handsome fellow. And his demeanor was much too meek for such a ferocious battle.

However, for 50 years William Wilberforce dedicated his life to the abolition of slavery. When he lay on his deathbed in 1833, a messenger appeared at his side. "Sir," the messenger whispered, "the abolition has been done and the parliament, right now, is bringing it to pass!"

Moments before he passed away, Wilberforce murmured his final few but powerful words: "I finished well."[4]

Digging Deeper: The Journey of Life with God

I love books that enlighten, encourage, and edify, giving me a definite sense that I have learned some valuable lesson(s) for my personal growth. It is my earnest desire that this book benefit you in similar ways. To this end, I encourage you while reading to keep in mind the following experiences and milestones in your life:

- your moment of salvation
- times of strength and growth with God
- your inner sense of destiny
- your understanding of God's call for your life

Then imagine your life as a home with many different rooms filled with different furnishings. Each room has its own character. You may consider some finished, while others are unfinished due to lack of time and resources. I invite you to consider the following "rooms" of your life:

- spiritual development
- marriage and family
- career and employment
- time spent alone with God
- character and holiness
- personal dreams and goals

If one or more of these rooms requires work or even needs to be built, you may want to make it a matter of prayer and, together with God, focus your energies there. Keep them in mind as you read this book, looking for God's will in how you should proceed.

You may even want to list some of these things on a 3" × 5" index card and slip it in your Bible. I often write insights I've had in my Bible. Some people I know use journals and even laptops to record their thoughts. Every person is different, so use the method that works best for you.

My prayer for you and my purpose for writing this book is to help you come to know and experience the will of God for your life and follow His will to its glorious end. May God speak to your heart as you read, pray, and consider His possibilities. "May [God] grant your heart's desire and fulfill all your plans" (Ps. 20:4 NLT).

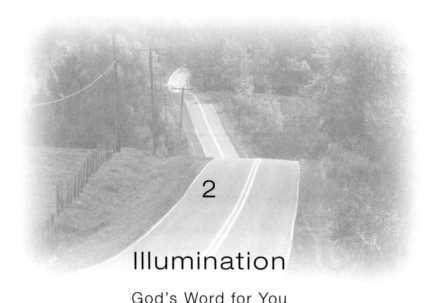

2

Illumination

God's Word for You

*Gaylord Kambarami, the General Secretary of the Bible
Society in Zimbabwe, tried to give a New Testament to a very
belligerent man. The man insisted he would roll the pages and
use them to make cigarettes. Mr. Kambarami said, "I
understand that, but at least promise to read the page of the
New Testament before you smoke it." The man agreed, and
the two went their separate ways. Fifteen years later, the two
men met at a Methodist convention in Zimbabwe. The
Scripture-smoking man had found Christ and was now a full-
time evangelist. He told the audience, "I smoked Matthew
and I smoked Mark and I smoked Luke. But when I got to
John 3:16, I couldn't smoke anymore. My life was changed
from that moment."[1]*

31

The centerpiece of God's will for you is found in His Word, the Bible. Don't let God's Word go up in smoke by failing to apply it to your life.

Thy word is a lamp unto my feet, and a light unto my path.

Psalm 119:105 KJV

THE BEST-SELLING BOOK of all time is the Bible. Although not everyone takes its words to heart, it is the most read book in history. Today historians tell us that Christianity—based on the Bible—has impacted human history more than all other religions of the world. That's because the Bible is much more than a book—it is the very Word of God!

Second Timothy 3:16 tells us: "All Scripture is given by inspiration of God, and is profitable for doctrine, for reproof, for correction, for instruction in righteousness." The Greek word for *inspiration* in the above verse means literally "breathed out by God" or simply "God-breathed." In short, God is the author of the Scriptures. He chose to pen His words through the hands of men, directing them by His Spirit. The biblical writers retained their personalities in their written communication, as well as their writing styles, but the message is from God Himself.

Some people have gone to great lengths to find errors and contradictions in the Bible. They have tried to disprove that the Bible is the verbally inspired Word of God. However, proof that the Scriptures are indeed authored by God is found in the impact this divine book has had on human life. The Bible has transformed more lives than any other person or resource in history. Perhaps there is no more sensational example of the life-transforming power of God's Word than the story of the mutiny on the *Bounty*.

In 1788, the *Bounty*, under Captain William Bligh, set sail for the island of Tahiti in the South Seas. After a voyage of ten months, the ship reached the Friendly Islands of Tonga, where the sailors became attached to the native girls. Upon receiving the order to embark in April 1788, the sailors mutinied, setting the captain and a few men adrift in an open boat while they returned to the island.

Captain Bligh survived the ordeal and eventually arrived home in England. A punitive expedition was sent out, which captured fourteen of the mutineers. But nine of them had transferred to another island, where they formed a new colony. Life in the colony degenerated rapidly. Whiskey was plentiful and, eventually, quarrels, orgies, and murders were an everyday occurrence.

Finally, all the men except one had been killed.

Alexander Smith was left alone with a crowd of native women and half-breed children. Then a strange thing happened. In a battered chest he found a Bible. He read it, believed it, and began to live it.

Determining to make amends for his past life of sin, he gathered the women and children around and taught them the Bible, too. As time passed, the children grew up and became Christians. The community prospered exceedingly. Nearly twenty years later, an American ship visited the island and brought back to Europe and England the word of its peaceful state.

The island was a Christian community. There was no disease, no insanity, no crime, no illiteracy, and no strong drink. Life and property were safe, and the moral standards of the people were higher than anyplace in the world. What had brought about this astounding transformation? Alexander Smith read one book. A divine book. The Bible.

Bringing the story up-to-date . . . In 1989, the King of Tonga—that same island where Alexander Smith was born again—invited some American pastors to go and baptize him as a Christian in a public ceremony on the island. When our pastors arrived in Tonga they found the island still had a large population of Christians. The power of the Bible that transformed Alexander Smith in 1788 was still having an impact over 200 years later.[2]

Only the Bible has the power to change people's lives, because it is the living Word of God. "For the LORD gives wisdom; from His mouth come knowledge and understanding" (Prov. 2:6). Few people realize that the Bible is the place to find God's will for their lives. Indeed, the Bible is God's love letter to you and to me; it contains thousands of answers to the questions of life, including:

- *Life-management skills.* Time management, crisis management, strategies for goal setting and achievement, use of innate gifts and spiritual gifts, career selection, and God's overall direction in your life can be found in the Bible.
- *Financial wisdom.* The Bible offers an enormous amount of insight concerning finances, managing money, investing, saving, and giving.
- *Relationships.* Friendship, love, forgiveness, communication, employer and employee relationships, even our responsibility toward government are all dealt with in the Bible.
- *Family.* The Bible includes principles for marital success; guidelines for raising children, conduct in the home, and purposeful living; and parameters for divorce.
- *Emotional health.* The Bible is the original textbook on positive thinking, emotional health, and achieving true inner peace.
- *Physical health.* Yes, the Bible even speaks about diet, physical health, and exercise.

So how do you find out about God's plan for your life? Look in His Word. The principles found there will give you the understanding you need for a fulfilling and exciting life. Remember, God does not want you to be confused or worried about life and the decisions you need to make. Sometimes you will need to wait on God, but He will always guide you to the end. As you apply the keys to knowing His will—as found in His Word—you will have success, but to get the maximum impact from God's Word, you need to make sure your heart is right with Him.

Second Timothy 2:15 says: "Be diligent to present yourself approved to God, a worker who does not need to be ashamed, rightly dividing the word of truth." The Greek word for *rightly dividing* is an ancient reference to cutting a straight line or a straight furrow, as a farmer does when planting corn. The ancient Greeks also used the word to describe the work of masons who cut marble so it fit precisely into block walls.[3] So, in the above verse, the words *rightly dividing* tell us to handle God's Word correctly.

Far too many people *mishandle* God's Word. Instead of allowing the Scriptures to mold and shape their lives, they allow the world to shape their lives—including their values, behaviors, beliefs, and lifestyles. God's Word is powerful. Through it you can grow in your knowledge of God, and by its power you will be conformed to the image of Christ.

Handling God's Word correctly includes the following practical applications:

Find a Bible-believing, Bible-teaching church. This is vital if God's Word is to have an impact on your heart and life. The better you know God's Word, the better able you will be to understand His will and live for Him.

Study the Bible. Learn the Word of God for yourself. The Bible is God's personal word to you. It is like an owner's manual, giving not only basic instruction but also very specific, personal guidance. Don't shy away from studying the Bible. It is written plainly and there are many translations and paraphrased versions that can help you easily understand the text. You will also find it helpful to have access to some of the good Bible study tools that are available today.

Depend on the Spirit of God. God's Spirit is the agent who will illumine your heart and mind regarding the truths of His Word. Pray and ask the Lord to give you understanding prior to reading Scripture. Then spend time meditating on verses that stand out to you, surveying the words and considering how they apply to your life. "Now we have received, not the spirit of the world, but the Spirit who is from God, that we might know the things that have been freely given to us by God" (1 Cor. 2:12).

Devotion: Developing a Life Plan

I am amazed at how diligently people study the things of the world. Ask most men about sports, for instance, and they can rattle off statistic after statistic, including championship teams, MVPs, game scores, and players from the past forty years. Ask most women where to get the best buy on a certain item and they can instantly give you a systematic rundown of every retail store and shopping mall in the area. People have knowledge about their areas of interest because they want to know and they make an effort to find out the details. Their devotion motivates their study.

If you want to know God's will for your life, which is revealed primarily in His Word, you *can* discover it—if you devote yourself to His Word. The old saying holds true: If you fail to plan, you are planning to fail. By planning to know God's Word, you are also planning to succeed by knowing His will for your life.

Invest the Time Wisely

King David said, "Oh, how I love your law! I think about it all day long. Your commands make me wiser than my enemies, for your commands are my constant guide" (Ps. 119:97–98 NLT). Consistent, sequential reading of the Bible is important if you want to begin to know it, and an outline that guides you through reading the Bible in one year (you will find such an outline at the end of this book) is extremely helpful. Mornings are a great time to read God's Word, because your mind is clear. The Scriptures often speak about seeking God early in the morning; however, if you are unable to read until lunchtime or evening, that's fine too. The important thing is finding time each day to read the Bible.

Not only can a daily reading plan be easy and enjoyable; it can transform your life. As most people consider beginning a daily reading program, however, they wonder where they will find the time. A recent survey revealed that the average American family spends two months per year watching TV. This means that every six years the average family has spent an entire year in front of the tube![4] Could that be why our nation is in crisis today? Please consider how you use your time. Devote some of it to reading God's Word and allowing Him the opportunity to unveil His will for your life. If you do, your life will be radically changed for the better.

Zero In

When I graduated from college many years ago, we were advised to enroll in a speed-reading program. I was—and still am—a slower reader than most people. However, my speed-reading class taught me some important lessons. First, nothing can take the place of normal-paced reading. Second, rereading a passage or meditating on a truth is extremely important. Believe me—it doesn't do any good to speed-read the Bible. I've tried it and learned it's just not profitable. Normal-paced reading with focus is absolutely indispensable as you begin to enjoy God's presence through His Word.

Joshua 1:8 says: "This Book of the Law shall not depart from your mouth, but you shall meditate in it day and night, that you may observe to do according to all that is written in it. For then you will make your way prosperous, and then you will have good success." As you meditate, focus, and study God's Word, He will speak to you through its timeless truths.

What's He Saying?

As you read the Scriptures, you can anticipate learning about God and hearing from Him. An old seminary saying reads, "The face of Christ is found on every page of His Book—the Bible." Speaking to the religious leaders of His day, Jesus said, "You search the Scriptures, for in them you think you have eternal life; and these are they which testify of Me" (John 5:39).

When you approach the Scriptures with a pure heart and right motives, does it mean you should expect to receive something personal from God? By all means, yes! Does it mean He will speak to you during the split second you get alone with Him? No. And getting fast answers should not be your sole objective for seeking God. People who go to Him with this motivation often get their priorities mixed up and, as a result, fail in times of decision and crisis.

Such was the case of a man living in Taiwan who was in love with a certain woman. Trying to win her heart, he wrote her seven hundred lengthy, flowery letters in one year, sixty-two of which included proposals of marriage. The letters worked. The lady did indeed get married—but not to him. She married the mailman!

After reading this story, I thought, *Isn't that just like us? The Father loves us and sends good gifts to us, and we're so dumb, we exalt the mailman instead of the One who sends the gifts.*

We get lured into the deceptive trap of looking for fast answers rather than spending time with God. We want the excitement of getting the mail—the special delivery—but we want to leave out the step where we meet with the Author of the letters who longs to spend time with us.

If you take the time to know God and His ways, when needs come, you will be well equipped to make wise, God-directed decisions. Certainly you should expect God to speak to you, but go to Him with the right motivation—love and devotion.

Listen Up

John 16:13 says: "However, when He, the Spirit of truth, has come, He will guide you into all truth; for He will not speak on His own authority, but whatever He hears He will speak; and He will tell you things to come." We often forget that the Spirit of God is the Third Person of the Trinity. And it's the Spirit who brings us into a deeper relationship with God. The Spirit of God will actually use His Word to touch your heart and direct your paths by giving you insight regarding your personal circumstances.

The Holy Spirit may give you a deep burden to begin praying for direction; He may convict you of sin so you can confess, repent, and move on; or He may bring a certain person to mind for whom you are to pray. When the Spirit of God speaks to you as you read your Bible and pray, take joy in responding. This is the exhilarating, Spirit-filled life—going with God wherever He leads. What could be more exciting?

As you read the Word of God, His Spirit will illuminate the Scriptures, and you will know what to do. As you spend time with God, you may experience a distinct impression in your heart or an inner prompting to take a certain action. Let me give you an example.

I recall a traumatic time in my life when I needed to make several major decisions, none for which I could find an easy answer in God's Word. After weeks of praying and searching for direction, worry began to grip me. I began lying awake at night in panic about the situations in my life. Then one morning as I read my Bible, the following psalm jumped off the page at me: "Unless the LORD builds the house, they labor in vain who build it; unless the LORD guards the city, the watchman stays awake in vain. It is vain for you to rise up early, to sit up late, to eat the bread of sorrows; for so He gives His beloved sleep" (Ps. 127:1–2).

What am I doing? I wondered. *I know this psalm, but I'm not living it! I'm not leaning on Him; I'm relying on myself.* God spoke to me through His Word regarding my personal situation. I realized He loved me and didn't want me losing sleep over my circumstances. He instructs us not to worry, not to be anxious. And I knew He would show me the answers to my problems as I continued to give Him the opportunity to lead me during quiet time with Him.

Needless to say, that night I slept like a rock. As I continued my daily devotional reading and prayer, over time, the answers to my concerns became crystal clear. What a faithful and personal God we serve! He is our friend and He wants to carry all our burdens for us.

He Lights the Way

"The entrance of Your words gives light; it gives understanding to the simple" (Ps. 119:130). God's plan is a treasure for your life. That plan is found in His Word, but you need to mine it for the treasures it contains. In time, as you continue in His Word, you will become more and more familiar with His will for you.

Psalm 119:93 says: "I will never forget Your precepts, for by them You have given me life." When you search the Scriptures for God's guidance, He will either answer your need directly with a passage from His Word that relates to your situation or answer indirectly by giving you divine principles from which you can formulate an answer.

When I was in college, I enrolled in a summer European tour. It was a whirlwind, twenty-one-nation trek through Europe in sixty days. Truly it was one of those journeys from which the saying must have been coined, "If this is Tuesday, it must be Brussels!"

The last stop of our tour was Rome. One of the places we visited was the world-famous catacombs, or tombs of the dead. The catacombs encompass miles of underground burial sites containing the remains of Christians who were tortured and killed, thrown to the lions, and burned alive by the notorious and bloodthirsty emperor Nero. Going forty feet underground by stairs, we came on a multitude of one-hundred-foot corridors, each illuminated by only one lightbulb and each lined with tombs of the dead. It seemed like the corridors never ended. The tour guides repeatedly warned us to stay on the lighted path. If we strayed off the lighted path, they warned, we could get lost for hours. So who do you think wandered from the light?

Yes, it was I. As my friends and I got carried away examining the Christian etchings on the tombs, we soon found ourselves separated from our light source and our tour group. Let me assure you, there is nothing more eerie than getting lost in the underground catacombs of Rome! It was pitch black and the dead surrounded us.

After some time, we were able to find a candle, light it, and work our way back to the group. If it weren't for the light, we never would have made it back.

In the same way, when we do not know God or His Word, we walk through life in darkness. And we are surrounded by death—in bondage to our sins and having no understanding of His will for our lives. However, when we come to the light of His Word, our path is illuminated.

God wants us to have a fruitful life. If you are lost, God's Word can help you find your way. If you have been waiting patiently for God to accomplish something in your life that hasn't happened yet (even though it may be happening in the lives of others around you), take joy in the fact that God has a plan for you that is good and beyond your imagination. If you are suffering right now according to the will of God, rejoice in the fact that it is for your good. He will answer you in His time.

Perhaps at this moment you are facing a particularly difficult struggle. I want you to know that either an explicit answer or principles you can follow can be found in the Bible. Perhaps you need to make a decision about a relationship or a financial situation and you have found the answer but are having difficulty following through. If so, pray and ask God to give you the strength to do what is right. God will be with you. And if you are afraid that you will make a mistake or a wrong decision, remember that even in failure God will be with you. You're His child. He knows you are vulnerable and prone to make mistakes. He wants to impart to you the wisdom necessary to navigate your life according to His direction.

Sir Walter Scott, a British poet and statesman, is known for the final words he spoke just before his death when he summoned his assistant and said, "Bring me the book." His assistant consented to Scott's request, but then challenged him by saying, "Sir Scott, you have many volumes in your library, which book shall I bring you?" Scott replied, "Bring me the book, the Bible, the only book for a dying man."[5]

All of us are dying and need to cling to God's Word for guidance.

Digging Deeper: Study the Bible

Set aside time to sit down, away from all distractions, and spend fifteen to thirty minutes in Bible study each day. Attempt to make your study a regular habit. If you like, use the reading plan at the back of this book and begin reading on today's date. If you're consistent and follow the plan, you'll have finished the Bible—from Genesis to Revelation (though not in that order)—one year from now.

You may want to purchase a Bible commentary that you can refer to when you have questions about certain Scriptures. Review the wide range of Bible study resources at your local Christian bookstore and choose one or two that will be helpful.

In His Word, God will show you His will and give you His promises, but you must be sure to test what you perceive to be His promises to confirm that they are from Him and that you are not just following your own will. When reading the Bible, keep a highlighter handy to mark those verses that really stand out to you. You may want to write dates next to the verses God uses to speak to you. Later, when the things happen that God pointed out, you can see from your notation when God first spoke His promise to you.

Finally, as you study the Bible, be open to God's prompting. He may lead you to stop and pray in the midst of your study or to worship Him in song or praise or by reading a psalm. If you don't pray and worship during your study, try to save a few minutes at the end to let God know how you feel about Him. Prayer and praise are all-important if you want to experience the joy of God's Spirit and the peace that comes from knowing Him personally.

"Study this Book of the Law continually. Meditate on it day and night so you may be sure to obey all that is written in it. Only then will you succeed" (Josh. 1:8 NLT).

3

Power

Plugging into Prayer

From the crest of the hill we saw it, like a vast scar on the green German landscape; a city of low gray barracks surrounded by concrete walls on which guard towers rose at intervals. In the very center, a square smokestack emitted a thin gray vapor into the blue sky.

"Ravensbruck!"

Like a whispered curse, the word passed back through the lines. This was the notorious women's extermination camp. At last, they drove us back from the faucets and herded us down an avenue between barracks. This camp appeared far grimmer than the one we had left. . . .

Betsie needed [her] sweater! She needed [her] vitamins! Most of all, we needed our Bible. How could we live in this place

45

*without it? But how could I ever take it past so many watchful
eyes without the overalls covering it? "Dear God," I prayed,
"You have given us this precious Book; You have kept it
hidden through checkpoints and inspections, You have used it
for so many . . ."*

*We stood alone in the room where a few minutes later we
would return stripped even of the clothes on our backs. And
then we saw something else, stacked in the far corner, a pile of
old wooden benches. They were slimy with mildew, crawling
with cockroaches, but to me they seemed the furniture of
heaven itself. "The sweater! Take the sweater off," I hissed,
fumbling with the string at my neck. Betsie handed it to me,
and in an instant I had wrapped it around the Bible and the
vitamin bottle, and stuffed the precious bundle behind the
benches.*

*We stood beneath the spigots as long as the flow of icy water
lasted, feeling it soften our lice-eaten skin. Then we clustered
dripping wet around the heap of prison dresses, holding them
up, passing them about, looking for approximate fits. I found
a loose long-sleeved dress for Betsie that would cover the blue
sweater when she would have a chance to put it on. I
squirmed into another dress myself, then reached behind the
benches and shoved the little bundle quickly inside the neck.*

*It made a bulge you could have seen across the Grote Market
(market plaza). I flattened it out as best I could, pushing it
down, tugging the sweater around my waist, but there was no
real concealing it beneath the thin cotton dress. And all the
while I had the incredible feeling that it didn't matter, that this
was not my business, but God's. That all I had to do was walk
straight ahead. As we trooped back out through the shower
room door, the S.S. men ran their hands over every prisoner,*

46

front, back and sides. The woman ahead of me was searched three times. Behind me, Betsie was searched.

No hand touched me.[1]

The incredible history of Corrie and Betsie ten Boom's living nightmare in Adolf Hitler's Nazi concentration camp wonderfully illustrates God's direct intervention into our lives through the agency of prayer.

We . . . do not cease to pray for you, and to ask that you may be filled with the knowledge of His will in all wisdom and spiritual understanding.

Colossians 1:9

ARE YOU WAITING for God to answer an urgent prayer? Perhaps you have been praying for something and hoping—even dreaming—that the answer would come, but you've not heard from God. You may find yourself wondering why. *Why hasn't God answered my prayer?*

In the verse from Colossians the apostle Paul tells us that we *can* pray to be filled with the knowledge of God's will. The word *filled* in this verse means "to be controlled by." A contemporary reading of this same verse gives us further insight into how prayer enables you to know God's will for your life: "We ask God to give you a complete understanding of what he wants to do in your lives, and we ask him to make you wise with spiritual wisdom" (Col. 1:9 NLT).

How can you know God's will for your life? Through prayer God fills us—literally controls us—with the knowledge of His will.

Almost sixty years ago, a young missionary named V. Raymond Edmond staggered from an Ecuadorian jungle into a medical clinic. He was desperately ill. The doctor, after examining him, predicted he would be dead by morning. Edmond's wife dyed her wedding dress black so it would be ready for the funeral. However, thousands of miles away in Boston, Edmond's friend, Dr. Joseph Evans, interrupted a prayer meeting and said, "I feel we must pray for V. Raymond Edmond in Ecuador." The group prayed earnestly until finally Evans called out, "Praise the Lord! The victory is won!"

V. Raymond Edmond recovered and went on to become the president of Wheaton College. His ministry lasted more than forty years.[2]

This beautiful story confirms the power of prayer and the will of God. The Lord had plans for V. Raymond Edmond, and He put it in the heart of a faithful friend in Boston to intercede on his behalf—through prayer.

God sometimes gives us an inner prompting to know His will in a matter. Just as He did in the dramatic account of Dr. Evans, God will often put a person on our heart at a particular time for us to intercede through prayer. If you feel a nudging or impression in your heart that you need to pray for someone, stop what you are doing and pray. It just may be that, as in the case of Dr. Evans, you will be interceding at a critical time.

Sometimes our prayers are practical—we go to God with our everyday needs. At other times our prayers reflect the deep needs of our heart, and sometimes our prayers consist of an anguished cry as we bring our difficult trials before the Lord.

The Bible tells us to pray in all situations. We need to ask God to fill us with the knowledge of His will for each day and each circumstance. Then we must trust that God will give us what we have asked for in prayer. On our knees we find the comfort and safety that only God can deliver.

George Adam Smith, a wonderful preacher and author, was on a mountain-climbing tour in the Alps. On one particularly high peak he ran to the pinnacle and looked out over Switzerland. Suddenly a strong gust of wind came up which threatened to blow him over the edge. From several feet away, his guide called to him, "Mr. Smith! On your knees, sir! The only way you're safe up here is on your knees!"[3]

I love the tremendous promise of John 15:7: "But if you stay joined to me and my words remain in you, you may ask any request you like, and it will be granted!" (NLT). It means that those impossible areas of my life can be solved by God's power through my prayer. Whether you are trying to overcome difficult sins, need money to pay the bills, are seeking employment, are in the process of repairing a damaged marriage, or need courage to witness to a friend—prayer is the key to unlocking God's will in your life.

You may have noted that there is a condition to unlocking the power of prayer. Jesus said, "If you stay joined to me . . ." The word *joined* is also rendered "abide" and means to stay in a certain relationship. The condition to receiving answers to prayer is to be joined to Jesus in a close relationship. Jesus went on with the condition, saying, ". . . and [if] my words remain in you . . ." God's Word is vital to your prayer life and influences your daily life. Jesus taught His disciples these two conditions for receiving answered prayer: Stay close to Me and let My Word be the central focus of your life. He asks us as well to meet these two conditions for answered prayer. If they are met, our prayers will be in accordance with His purposes and we will receive what we have asked for, according to His will.

Jesus said, "Until now you have asked nothing in My name. Ask, and you will receive, that your joy may be full" (John 16:24). Asking in Jesus's name means to ask in accordance with His nature, purpose, and divine will. To illustrate how this works, let me use a personal example. Let's say that my little eleven-year-old daughter, Chelsea, goes to the toy store and presents my charge card to buy a new pair of roller skates. When the cashier sees how young she is and that the name on the card is not hers, she might say, "Young lady, I must call your father and ask if he will permit you to charge these skates in his name." When I get the call, I would say, "Yes, we have discussed this purchase and I have given her my permission to buy them!" I give permission for my daughter to use my charge card and to purchase the skates in my name.

Now let's say that after visiting the toy store, Chelsea then wanders next door to a car dealership that specializes in exotic imported sports cars. She presents my credit card on the sales counter and asks to purchase the latest model Ferrari in fire-engine red. Immediately I receive a call from the salesman who asks if I will permit my daughter to buy the car. He says my daughter has told him to tell me that if I will permit her to buy the car, she will let me drive it until she is old enough to drive. My response is a resounding no. She does not have my permission to buy a Ferrari, and I will not let her use my card or my name as a guarantee. A Ferrari is not in my will for my daughter.

Although this illustration stretches reality, it nevertheless makes a good point. When we go to God in prayer and ask for something in Christ's name, we are saying, "Will You attach Your name to my desire?" Whether the desire is a new purchase, business venture, relationship, or idea, God will answer—according to His will.

You and I need to understand that not everything we desire is within God's will for our lives. God will grant only those requests that are in keeping with His divine will. We often think that we know what's best for our lives, but it is the Lord who knows what will bring us true joy and fulfillment. When we walk through this world abiding by God's will, we experience abundant life.

First John 5:14–15 says: "And we can be confident that he will listen to us whenever we ask him for anything in line with his will. And if we know he is listening when we make our requests, we can be sure that he will give us what we ask for" (NLT).

Perseverance with a Capital *P*

Experiencing power in prayer often has to do with perseverance. God's answers do not always come quickly. Scripture commands us to continue praying until the situation is resolved: "Rejoicing in hope, patient in tribulation, continuing steadfastly in prayer" (Rom. 12:12).

The challenge to continue in prayer is a most difficult undertaking for some believers. But those who take up the gauntlet and *continue* to pray always receive an answer.

Consider the following answer to prayer described by a grieving wife in Alabama:

Dear Abby,

Six years ago my husband of twenty-two years announced that he wanted a divorce and was moving out. Our eighteen-year-old son and I were crushed. I was in shock and didn't know what to do. Being a Christian, I began to pray and asked my friends to pray for my husband. Two months later my doorbell rang, and there stood my husband wanting to talk. We both sat down and cried like babies. He asked me to forgive him for the hurt he had caused me. He had realized that the grass was not greener on the other side of the fence. My advice to "Dying inside Missouri" and others going through the same situation is this: If you still love him, don't give up. Pray instead. It really works.

Persevering faith enables us to continue in prayer. If we believe God and His Word, we never give up praying. However, if we harbor unbelief in our heart, we will easily give up when there appears to be silence from heaven.

Have you ever felt you had a problem or trial that was impossible to correct? God takes the impossible situations in our lives and by His power makes them right. Perhaps you have a besetting sin that you feel helpless to conquer. God's power smashes habitual sins into pieces. Maybe you are in the midst of a dire situation that you feel is unbearable. God turns disaster into wonderful blessings and mighty testimonies. Perhaps a loved one for whom you have been praying for many years still has not come to the Lord. There is *nothing* God cannot do. His power is not something that He holds back from us; instead, we need to access it. Tap into it. Keep on praying. God's timing is perfect. He *will* answer.

God's Peace in Prayer

Paul the apostle, when writing to the young church in Philippi, Greece, assured believers that prayer brings God's peace. He said, "Don't worry about anything; instead, pray about everything. Tell God what you need, and thank him for all he has done. If you do this, you will experience God's peace, which is far more wonderful than the human mind can understand" (Phil. 4:6–7 NLT).

The Greek word for *worry* in this verse means "to be pulled in different directions." The old English root from which we get our word *worry* means "to strangle." When we worry, we strangle so many areas of our lives. Our devotion to God suffers. We have trouble receiving His divine direction. Our personal creativity suffers, and our strength is depleted. Life becomes dull and difficult.

In 1929, business tycoon J.C. Penney was hospitalized for severe anxiety. One night he was sure he was going to die, so he wrote farewell letters to his wife and son. But he survived the night, and hearing singing the next morning in the chapel, felt drawn to go in. A group was singing, "God Will Take Care of You," after which followed Bible reading and prayer.

Penney said, "Suddenly something happened. I can't explain it. It was a miracle. I felt as if I had been instantly lifted out of the darkness of the dungeon into warm brilliant sunlight. I felt as if I had been transported from hell to paradise. I felt the power of God as I had never felt it before.

"I realized then that I alone was responsible for all my troubles. I knew that God with His love was there to help me. From that day to this, my life has been free from worry. The most dramatic and glorious minutes of my life were those I spent in that chapel that morning."[4]

What is the opposite of worry? It's peace. When we have the peace of God, our life is fresh, full of vitality, overflowing with living water, and in constant communion with Him. Peace comes from God. When you become a Christian, you have peace with God. You are no longer in opposition to Him, but instead you are reconciled to God and have a relationship with Him. God's peace floods your mind, even when outward circumstances appear hopeless. Philippians 4:7 tells us that God's peace "garrisons your mind." This is a military term that means protection from outside distractions such as anxiety, fear, and anger.

Why is it that we often do not possess God's peace in our lives? Many times it is because our prayer life falls short of God's design. Even after we have confessed the sin in our life that separates us from God's peace, we may still feel anxious. Do you realize that an overly busy schedule, a lack of physical exercise, an improper diet, and many other factors will also affect your peace?

God desires that prayer be a constant part of each day. Prayer is important, whether we are at home, at work, enjoying a fun day out, or on vacation. God desires to communicate with us through prayer and to bless us in the process with the experience of knowing His will. Jeremiah 33:3 says:

"Call to Me, and I will answer you, and show you great and mighty things, which you do not know."

I once heard an interviewer ask Dr. Billy Graham about his prayer life. Dr. Graham said that he always prayed throughout each day, and he then said to the interviewer, "I am even praying now at this very moment during this interview."

The life that God blesses with spiritual power and divine direction is one bathed in prayer and ultimately makes the difference between a life fraught with worry and a life bathed in peace. "For the mind set on the flesh is death, but the mind set on the Spirit is life and peace" (Rom. 8:6 NASB).

Robert Strand tells this story, which he read in a surgical magazine, about a hard-pressed, irritable, nervous, overworked surgeon in a busy New York City hospital and the power of peace.

> The doctor was ready to perform another emergency operation. He was in a hurry, it was Christmas Eve, and it had been quite a day in the surgical suite.
>
> The patient was a beautiful girl of seventeen who had been seriously injured in an auto accident. The nurse, about to give the anesthetic, said kindly, "Relax, breathe deeply, and the pain will be gone." The girl said, "Would you mind if I repeated the twenty-third psalm from the Bible, before you operate?"
>
> The nurse looked at the surgeon and he nodded; the girl began: "The Lord is my Shepherd, I shall not want . . ." The surgeon continued with his preparations, but everyone else stood still, listening. They had heard these beautiful words many times in church, but they had never sounded so moving. Here in that surgical suite, they had another meaning, a deeper, very real meaning.
>
> The girl went on, "Though I walk through the valley of the shadow of death, I will fear no evil, for Thou art with me . . ."
>
> The nurse held the cone above her to begin with the anesthetic. "Hold it," said the doctor, "Let her finish." Then he

moved over and looked down at her and said, "Go on, honey, say it to the end and say it for me, too, won't you?"

They all stood quietly and listened as her heart, full of faith, filled the operating room that Christmas Eve day. They heard some of the most moving words ever written: "Thy rod and Thy staff they comfort me," she paused, catching her breath, then went on to the finish, "and I will dwell in the house of the Lord forever."

The surgeon looked down at her. He was relaxed—his sense of irritation was gone. There was no feeling of other duties pressing in on him. He and his patient and the operating room crew were at peace and ready for the surgery.[5]

One Step Ahead of Us

"I will answer them before they even call to me. While they are still talking to me about their needs, I will go ahead and answer their prayers!" (Isa. 65:24 NLT).

Several years ago I was asked to teach some Bible students in India. This was my first trip there, and it took more than fifty hours to reach the southern tip of India, near Sri Lanka. To get to the city where the ministry headquarters were located, the other pastors and I had to take a bus ride that lasted hours. Needless to say, when we got to our destination, we were dead tired, having slept only a few hours during the journey.

At the headquarters we were able to get about four hours of sleep. Then, at 5:00 a.m., a guide took three of us in a jeep to an outlying village, well into the jungle. We drove four hours, past elephants and other wildlife. When we arrived in the village, we saw a massive hut. About three hundred Indian students were inside, beating drums and singing loudly. It seemed like something out of a Hollywood movie; in my half-awake state, I felt like I was dreaming.

Before the jeep stopped, the guide asked, "Okay, which of you is going to speak?" I said to myself, *Did he say "sleep"?* The last thing I wanted to do was speak!

I was sitting in the back of the jeep, with my eyes half closed, and the other guys said, "Gary, you've done this before. Why don't you go ahead and speak?"

"Great," I said, less than enthusiastically. "Thanks a lot, guys."

On our way to the giant thatched hut where the students were singing, we walked past a little headquarters building, and out of the corner of my eye, I saw a small table on which was sitting one of those old, red American telephones with a rotary dial. As I glanced at the phone and wondered what it was doing there, it began to ring!

Have you ever had a gut feeling something was going to happen—and it did? Well, I had a gut feeling that this telephone call was for me. Smiling, I thought, *It's probably my wife.*

An Indian gentleman ran over and answered the phone. He then looked at me and asked, "Are you Gary?"

I walked apprehensively toward the phone, knowing I had to address this big group in less than two minutes. Sure enough, it was my wife. I said, "How on earth did you contact me here, and why of all times now?"

She answered, "Honey, it took me hours to get connected . . . I have some bad news."

Then one of my worst fears—that something would happen to one of my children—was realized. My wife was calling to tell me that our son was in the emergency room in critical condition due to an allergic reaction to medication. I felt totally helpless. I was halfway around the world and could not be there with my wife and son. Fear and sadness gripped my heart as I tried to console my wife over the phone.

I knew the only thing I could do was pray—and pray fervently. I hung up the phone and walked into the giant thatched hut. My translator, who was standing near the door, asked me what was wrong. I told him my son was very sick. The translator said, "Now you just sit down. We are prayer warriors. Wait for us."

As I sat down, he announced to the students that my son was very sick and they needed to pray. Instantly the crowd began to pray powerfully in unison. I was moved as I watched more than three hundred students in a little remote village in India intercede on my son's behalf through prayer.

Let me tell you—the power of prayer wrought a miracle. The very next day I found out my son was healed. God used believers in India to intercede with God, who healed a little boy halfway around the world! Extraordinary things happen when God's people pray.

In the 1700s and 1800s, there were three great periods of spiritual awakening in the United States that kept our nation from certain disaster and destruction. Millions of people were converted, and our nation survived war and disunity. Similarly, across the Atlantic Ocean, in Wales, so awesome was the effect of conversion that in certain villages, bars and houses of prostitution closed down due to a lack of business.

What brought on this mass conversion? Extraordinary prayer. Ordinary people like you and me came together in Christ and began to pray. This principle of prayer is something you can make use of in your own life. Your life can be changed—as can the lives of those around you—when you set your heart and mind on prayer.

God's Blueprint for Prayer

Sometimes you and I don't realize what we're missing. God longs to pour out His blessings in our lives in response to our prayers, but we pray so little. How is it that we have time to go to the gym, watch TV, shop, and go to restaurants, but we seldom have time to pray? We may say an obligatory prayer before our meals or in church, but rarely do we spend concentrated time praying over our lives and the lives of others.

What's wrong? Why do we neglect to pray? I believe it's because we look at prayer as boring and futile. In our society we've been trained to devote ourselves to activities that bring results. And we want *instant* results!

James 4:2 says: "The reason you don't have what you want is that you don't ask God for it" (NLT). When you pray as God intends, you will get results. God's blueprint for prayer consists of six key elements: solitude, worship, Scripture, thanksgiving, confession, and expressing our desires. Let's look at each one. Even if you are a seasoned prayer warrior, these keys can revolutionize and revitalize your prayer life.

Solitude

Prayer requires total concentration, away from daily distractions. Find a time and place where you can be alone. This may require that you get up early or stay up late. The Scriptures make many references to rising early in the morning for prayer. Two reasons for this are that early mornings are quiet and offer the solitude you need, before the hustle and bustle of the day begins; and prayer time is a blessed way to start your day, communing with the Lord, giving Him your burdens, and talking with Him about your agenda and tasks for the day.

Just as spending time with your mate establishes a loving bond between you, taking time alone with God is vital for the health of your relationship with Him. How about going on an outing with God? Go to a park, the beach, or the mountains and spend time alone with Him. Pour out your heartfelt needs, innermost feelings, and deepest desires. God enjoys this interaction with you and will often impart His will to you during these times. "I love those who love me, and those who seek me diligently will find me" (Prov. 8:17).

Worship

In the minds of many people, prayer involves telling God what they need—similar to picking up the telephone and ordering a pizza, then hanging up! But prayer should be much more than that. Prayer is about communicating with God and nurturing your relationship with Him. Imagine if your best friend or spouse called you to tell you his or her deepest dreams, needs, and problems, and afterward, when you were ready to share your feelings, your friend or spouse said, "Okay, it felt good to unload. I've got to go now. It was nice talking to you!" Would you be frustrated? Of course, because this is a relationship based not on love but on self-ishness. Yes, prayer includes voicing your needs to God, but it should also be a time when we hear from Him.

Devotion to God, straight from the heart, is powerful. We should choose to worship the Lord through song, prayer, and praise. Psalm 95:1 says: "Come, let us sing to the LORD! Let us give a joyous shout to the rock of our salvation!" (NLT). Indeed, it's vital that our prayer time includes our worship of God—acknowledging and giving thanks for who He is and for what He has done in our lives. Worship also involves the all-important discipline of waiting on the Lord in silence. Often in these times, God will flood our minds with His love, peace, joy, and divine guidance. It is not un-usual for waiting to happen spontaneously as we worship God, and it is during these sweet times that He may give answers to our prayers.

For those of you who are exceptionally busy, trying to make ends meet financially or raising a motley crew of kids, take heart. God can speak to you when your energy level is down and when your time is sparse as well.

Scripture

As covered in chapter 1, Scripture is indispensable to your understanding of God and His will for your life, but did you know that Scripture can be a part of your prayer life as well? We need to remember to thank God in prayer for His Word and ask Him to speak to us through our daily devotional reading. "Let my cry come before You, O LORD; give me understanding according to Your word" (Ps. 119:169).

There are more than one thousand promises to believers found in the Word of God. How important is it then that we take these promises, apply them to our lives, and remind ourselves and God of them during our prayer time! "I wait for the LORD, my soul waits, and in His word I do hope" (Ps. 130:5).

Prayer and God's Word go hand in hand, and our Bible reading and prayer time will have more power in our lives if we are careful to keep them together.

Thanksgiving

Think about your life. Is there a great deal for which you are thankful? If you're like me, you may sometimes grumble about what you don't have. Remember, however, to thank and praise God for all you do have—your breath, abilities, senses, provisions, family, friends, church, salvation, and so much more. Above all, we need to be thankful that God is loving, merciful, and faithful. Psalm 106:1 says: "Praise the LORD! Give thanks to the LORD, for he is good! His faithful love endures forever" (NLT).

Do you realize that your spiritual and emotional health is revitalized when you come to God in thanksgiving? It's true. You'll notice yourself becoming stronger as you learn to dwell on His power instead of your own anxieties.

Confession

One of the most important of all spiritual disciplines is confession. You can go to God in confidence and pour out your heart and innermost feelings concerning your failure and sin. Remember, to have an effective prayer life and a right relationship with the Lord, you need to confess your sins to Him.

As soon as you become aware of a sin, bring it to God, asking Him to cleanse you with the blood of Christ and to grant forgiveness. We are not to be careless about our sins. Psalm 66:18 states: "If I regard iniquity in my heart, the Lord will not hear."

God is gracious and merciful. He is always willing to forgive those with hearts set on Him. This forgiveness paves the way for a new start in the day and opens the windows of heaven for His blessings to flow. "If we confess our sins, He is faithful and righteous to forgive us our sin and to cleanse us from all unrighteousness" (1 John 1:9 NASB).

Remember too that repentance follows confession. A determined mind and heart coupled with God's Spirit are the key to repentance. If you are struggling with a particular sin, ask God for the cleansing blood of Christ to forgive and for His power to change.

Often confession and repentance open new doors for God's work in our lives. We should be aware that many people seeking God's will have experienced change as a result of forsaking sin. Marriages have been healed, families reconciled, businesses set back on track, and doors for service opened wide.

Desires

Praying about their desires is not a problem for most Christians. I have placed it last in my list of key elements of prayer, not for any biblical reason, but because putting our desires last can inspire us to faith. What I mean is, once we have gotten alone with God, worshiped Him, read His Word, thanked Him, and confessed our sins, we will have a much better perspective on our needs and desires. Then we can approach God with a humble heart, wanting God's way above our own.

Desires generally come in two areas—personal needs and the needs of others. Your personal prayer requests may include daily provisions, job needs, help with a relationship, strength to carry on in life, power to change, or the ability to live for God in the midst of struggle. You can bring *anything* to God in prayer, however major or trivial! God is concerned about it all.

When it comes to the needs of others, the Lord wants you to pray for these as well. This is commonly called intercessory prayer. Bringing others' needs to God is as important as praying about your own needs.

If you happen to be in the midst of a difficult situation and you don't know what to do, keep praying and seeking His will! God wants to move in your life. No matter how impossible your situation may seem, He can turn it around and use it for good.

Many times God will take care of your predicament without your getting involved. I love it when I don't have to do anything about a situation—except pray! God takes care of it all. He has supernatural ways of solving problems without our help. The following story, as told by Rev. H. C. Morrison, illustrates this well.

Bishops Lambeth and Wainwright had a mission meeting in Osaka, Japan. One day the order came from Japanese officials that Christian meetings were no longer allowed in the city. Lambeth and Wainwright did all they could, but the officials were unrelenting. The bishops then retired to the prayer room. Suppertime arrived and a Japanese servant girl came to summon them to their meal but found herself falling under the power of prayer. Mrs. Lambeth, wondering why no one had come to dinner, went to the prayer room and she fell under the same power. The group then rose, went to the mission hall, and immediately started a prayer meeting.

God worked a miracle through the prayers of the believers, causing two sons of the city officials to come to the altar and be converted. The next morning one of the officials in authority came to the mission and said, "Go on with your meeting, you will not be interrupted."

The Osaka daily paper came out with the headline: "The Christians' God Came to Town Last Night."

I want you to know that today God can visit your town, home, workplace, and personal life. His plans are always grand. He still works miracles in everyday ways, so don't stop praying. Prayer will tap you into the supernatural and bring you into alignment with God's will. Let God work in your life in the remarkable ways He has planned.

Digging Deeper: How about a Date?

Seek out that special location where you can get alone with God. Meet Him there. In time, you will look forward to this time with God as you would a date with a loved one, because that's exactly what it is. This will be your hiding place where God can meet with you, and you with Him.

On your date, include Bible reading, asking God to illuminate the Scriptures as you read. Sometimes, during your reading, God will speak a promise or a command to you from a passage—it can touch your soul. Then use that Scripture in your prayer time.

Pour your heart out to God. At first, it may seem a bit awkward. But don't let embarrassment detour you from this life-changing discipline. God will honor your prayers. He loves a humble heart.

Write the deepest desires of your heart in your journal, specifically those things that come to you in deep prayer. Make note of the date that you prayed, and then, when God answers—whether with a yes or no or by way of an open or closed door—note His response. Also, write your feelings about what happened.

Remember, prayer is not only talking to God, it is also waiting in silence to hear from Him. "My soul, wait silently for God alone, for my expectation is from Him" (Ps. 62:5). The Bible discusses a still, small voice, a peace that surpasses understanding, and an impression on your heart. God will speak to you in a variety of ways.

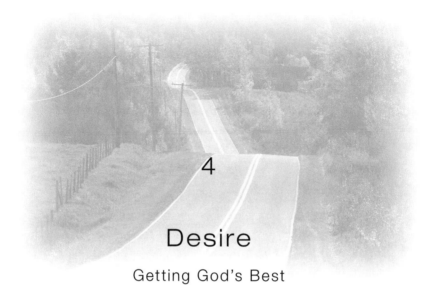

4

Desire

Getting God's Best

In 1924 at the Paris Olympic Games, Eric Liddell stirred his generation not only with an ultimate victory in the 400-meter dash, but more importantly, by refusing to race on Sunday to honor God. The entire story was depicted in the Academy Award–winning film Chariots of Fire. *If you saw it, you will remember the surprise you felt when at the end of the movie you read these words about the hero:*

"Eric Liddell, missionary, died in occupied China at the end of World War II. All of Scotland mourned."

Exactly one year after winning the gold medal, Eric Liddell went to China as a missionary with the London Missionary Society. After teaching at a college there, he decided to engage in rural evangelism. Whether by bicycle or by foot, Liddell carried the Gospel of Jesus Christ to the backcountry of China.

After Japan invaded China, Liddell was classified as an "enemy national," and in August 1943 he was sent to a prison camp. He was one of 1,800 prisoners packed into a facility that measured 150 by 200 yards. He was housed in a dormitory that provided a room three feet by six feet for each man. While a prisoner, Liddell accepted the challenge of his situation and organized athletic meets, taught hymns, and ministered God's Word.

David Mitchell was a child imprisoned with Liddell. He later remembered the influence this national hero had upon everyone in the prison. Mitchell stated, "None of us will ever forget this man who was totally committed to putting God first—a man whose humble life combined muscular Christianity with radiant godliness."

Just months before he would have been liberated, on February 21, 1945, Eric Liddell died of a brain tumor. He was not only a national hero, but a hero of the faith. Indeed, his life and testimony continue to inspire others to follow Christ to this day.[1]

At the end of *Chariots of Fire*, as Eric is running the four hundred meters, his words can be heard: "When I run, I feel His pleasure." God has created us with wonderful desires that He alone can fulfill. Realizing His will for your life also means fulfilling your greatest desires.

Eric Liddell was a man who loved to run. His heart's desire was fulfilled in an extraordinary way, because God chose Eric Liddell for the task of bringing Him glory.

Delight yourself also in the LORD, and He shall give you the desires of your heart.

Psalm 37:4

IS IT POSSIBLE that God will give you the desires of your heart? I have often asked this question. Believe it or not, the answer is found in the very complexity and beauty of God's creation. Take a walk in a field and examine just one beautiful flower crafted by God. You will find countless extraordinary characteristics about that flower. Since God puts so much effort into the details of one flower, don't you think He can bring His glorious will and your most intimate desires together in one fulfilling life?

Jesus said, "And if God cares so wonderfully for flowers that are here today and gone tomorrow, won't he more surely care for you? You have so little faith!" (Luke 12:28 NLT).

The life of John Coltrane, the great saxophonist who played with Dizzy Gillespie and Miles Davis, illustrates the power of God to fulfill our deepest desires as we delight in Him.

In the early 1950s, "Trane" nearly died of a drug overdose in San Francisco. When he recovered, he quit drugs and drinking, and put his faith in God. After his conversion, Trane produced some of his best jazz, including "A Love Supreme," an ardent, 32-minute outpouring to God that was filled with thanksgiving and adoration.

After an extraordinary live rendition of "A Love Supreme," Coltrane stepped off the stage, put down his saxophone, and simply said, *"Nunc dimittus."* The ancient Latin words are translated: "Lord, now lettest thou thy servant depart in peace, for mine eyes have seen thy salvation."

Coltrane felt he could never play the piece more perfectly. If his whole life had been lived for that passionate 32-minute jazz prayer, it would have been worth it. He was ready to go.[2]

If you are open and your heart is fixed on God, He can do fantastic things in your life. He can fulfill your deepest dreams and desires.

What is the key to the fulfillment of your desires? Delighting yourself in the Lord! The word *delight* (Ps. 37:4) in the original language means "to be soft or pliable"—flexible to the ways of God. The Lord wants you to be open and moldable to His ways. Are you like putty in the hands of God?

Delighting in the Lord means trusting Him with all of your heart, even in the midst of the most difficult circumstances.

Delighting in the Lord means dwelling in your circumstances with His joy.

Delighting in the Lord means committing your life to Him, including the most practical aspects of your daily routines.

Are you delighting in the Lord? The answer to this question may reveal the nature of your desires.

When you take your eyes off yourself and begin to focus entirely on God, a wonderful thing happens. Your joy begins to increase. This is the result of delighting in the Lord, and this was the secret of King David's life, when he said, "I delight to do Your will, O my God, and Your law is within my heart" (Ps. 40:8).

Living life God's way is more rewarding than pursuing the most grandiose plans without Him. Because your heavenly Father made you for a purpose, He knows what's best for you, and it is only when you yield to His will that you will experience a fulfilled life.

Bank on It—God's Plan Is Best

"Trust also in Him, and He shall bring it to pass" (Ps. 37:5). The word *trust* means "to be sure, bold, secure"—to place your entire confidence in God. Trusting God with your life is critical to receiving the desires of your heart. Most people consider three things before trusting in God— money, means, and men. But when they trust these things before God, they always come up unfulfilled and lacking contentment.

> In May of 1995, Randy Reed, a 34-year-old construction worker, was welding on a nearly completed water tower near Chicago. According to one writer, Randy had unhooked his safety gear to reach some pipes and as he did, a metal cage slipped and bumped the scaffolding on which Reed was standing. He slipped and was launched 110 feet down to the earth. He fell face down in a pile of dirt barely missing rocks and construction debris. When the paramedics arrived, Reed was breathing. When they hoisted him on the backboard and carried him to the ambulance, he actually spoke.
>
> What did the man who lived after free-falling 110 feet have to say to the paramedics who were transporting him?
>
> "Please, don't drop me!"[3]

Do you fear that if you place your life completely in the hands of God, He may drop you? Why do we fear giving the Lord total control over our lives? Are we afraid of what He might permit to happen?

Think about it. The idea of not being able to trust the infinite and sovereign Creator of the universe is ridiculous, isn't it? Nevertheless, one of the most difficult bridges to cross in knowing the will of God is trusting that *His plan is better than our own.*

Why should you put your complete trust in God?

- God is wonderful, and His will is more glorious than anything on earth.
- God is the Creator, and His plan is the only one that will fulfill the purposes for which you were created.
- God is in total control of the universe. He is the only One who can miraculously guide you to the destiny He has chosen for you.
- God commands you to trust Him, because He loves you and wants to accomplish His will in your life.

Therefore, the most important thing in life that you can do is surrender. Give your anxiety to God. Let it go. Place every ounce of your confidence in God—the One who knows all things about your life and can bring glorious things to pass. Remember He will never drop you.

When adversity comes, our trust is tested. In the middle of the fire of tribulation, we often want to retreat. However, God is in the midst of the flames and will keep us going during the most difficult times.

One of the most vivid examples in Scripture of the need to trust God in the midst of adversity is the experience of Daniel's three friends in the fiery furnace.

Nebuchadnezzar, the king of Babylon, sentenced Daniel's friends—Shadrach, Meshach, and Abednego—to death for refusing to worship an idol. The king decreed that they be thrown into a fiery furnace where they would burn to death. The king was so aggravated by the insolence of these three fearless Yahweh believers that he ordered his soldiers to heat the furnace seven times hotter than normal. The heat was so intense that some of the soldiers died as they approached the furnace to throw Shadrach, Meshach, and Abednego into the flames.

But something remarkable happened.

"'Look!' Nebuchadnezzar shouted. 'I see four men, unbound, walking around in the fire. They aren't even hurt by the flames! And the fourth looks like a divine being!'" (Dan. 3:25 NLT).

Nebuchadnezzar ordered the three young men to come out of the furnace. To the utter astonishment of the king, not a hair on their heads was burned. A new edict went forth from the king telling the people of the land to worship the God of Shadrach, Meshach, and Abednego, and because of their trust in God in the face of adversity, these three men received a promotion. Even the king became a believer!

You are never alone in the midst of adversity and suffering. God is right there with you, and He has promised that the adversity will actually work for your benefit—there is always a reason for it (see Rom. 8:28). As you trust Him, you will find that He will protect you in the midst of the trial and bless you.

Perhaps you are suffering through a situation that you really don't understand. You are asking why this is happening to you. God doesn't always give an explanation for what He is doing or allowing in your life. However, He has promised that He will not allow anything in your life you cannot handle (see 1 Cor. 10:13).

Habakkuk 1:5 says: "For I am doing something in your own day, something you wouldn't believe even if someone told you about it" (NLT). When you understand that the trials of life are actually preparing you for the grand plans God has for your future, you will come to trust all of His ways and means.

Be Patient—God Is at Work

You have probably heard the cliché "Bloom where you are planted." In a real sense, this is what God is asking you to do in your life. Are you unhappy in your current circumstances? Do bitterness and remorse haunt you? Are you depressed and anxious about the future? God wants you to trust that your present circumstances are directly in line with His divine plan. God wants to bless you right where you are.

"Dwell in the land, and feed on His faithfulness" (Ps. 37:3). In this verse, the word *dwell* comes from a root word meaning "to lie down, sleep, take rest and be still, and to continue permanently." At times God permits us to remain in certain difficult situations. The fact is, the Bible says trials cause you to grow strong in character; they prepare you for the work God has for you to do. Through it all, God wants you to understand that He loves you and is working His best for you.

The ancient Hebrew word translated *feed* in the verse is *ra'ah*, which means "to graze, devour, eat up, and feed," as well as "to keep company and associate with (as a friend)." The idea of faithfulness is also contained in the word *feed*, where it refers to a shepherd who takes care of his flock. In essence, God is the Good Shepherd who places us in the right pastures, divinely appointed from the foundation of the world.

You may be questioning the pasture God has placed you in at this time, but when you feed on His faithfulness, worshiping Him and staying in His Word, you will find great comfort for your heart, no matter what your circumstances. This is what it means to dwell with God. You can make a rose garden out of a patch of thorns if you dwell with Him and learn His ways.

The story of Mary and Martha illustrates the importance of dwelling with God:

> As Jesus and the disciples continued on their way to Jerusalem, they came to a village where a woman named Martha welcomed them into her home. Her sister, Mary, sat at the Lord's feet, listening to what he taught. But Martha was

worrying over the big dinner she was preparing. She came to Jesus and said, "Lord, doesn't it seem unfair to you that my sister just sits here while I do all the work? Tell her to come and help me."

But the Lord said to her, "My dear Martha, you are so upset over all these details! There is really only one thing worth being concerned about. Mary has discovered it—and I won't take it away from her."

Luke 10:38–42 NLT

Mary discovered that the most important thing was to get to know Jesus by sitting at his feet and spending time with Him. Before you can know God's will for your life, you must come to know God Himself.

To emphasize that point, think about the beautiful, life-size granite carving of Jesus Christ by Danish sculptor Thors Walden. Walden sculpted the body of Christ in such a way that you cannot see His face from a standing position. But a sign next to the statue reads: "If you want to see the face of Jesus, you must sit at his feet."[4]

Revelation and adoration are intricately linked together. When you are at the feet of Jesus Christ in worship, you will see things that others do not.

Leave It to Him

Earlier I quoted Psalm 37:5: "Trust also in Him, and He shall bring it to pass." Here is the beginning of the verse: "Commit your way to the LORD." The word *commit* means literally "to roll your way to the Lord" and carries the meaning of treading a path. It is a direct reference to the paths of life. This word also conveys the idea of rolling a heavy burden from you to another—in our case, laying it on God so He can bear it.

Did you know that you have the freedom to pursue your dreams, provided you are committed to God?

NASCAR driver Ned Jarrett, who won the Winston 500 Cup, said, "I was put here for a reason and it wasn't just to run races."[5] Ned is a committed Christian, and his mission is to reach people for Jesus Christ.

When our first priority is God, our dreams are governed by our desire to please Him. We can dream dreams and we can love God. This winning combination produces an abundant and purposeful life.

Be Available

It's God's desire that you commit your plans and conduct to Him daily. Commitment begins in the morning with prayer and continues throughout the day as you encounter all He has for you.

As you wake up in the morning, ready to get out of bed, you may want to offer up a prayer something like this: "God, I am available for You today. Direct me and intercede in my schedule, plans, and life as You desire. Help me hear from You and joyfully follow. Help me be Your representative today. Glorify Your name through me."

God wants you to place the plans you have for your life into His hands. This is the only way to have a true and meaningful life. When you make God your top priority, everything else will fall into place. Jesus said, "'You shall love the LORD your God with all your heart, with all your soul, and with all your mind.' This is the first and great commandment" (Matt. 22:37–38).

Where God Guides, He Provides

It's been said that God's will is like walking through a tunnel with a flashlight, which lights the path immediately in front of us. Occasionally, however, God lifts the flashlight to give us a glimpse of what the future holds. Those glimpses into the future can really inspire us.

As you commit your way to God, ask yourself if you strongly sense His leading and direction. Remember, your senses are not perfect, but God's ways are. "I will instruct you and teach you in the way you should go; I will guide you with My eye" (Ps. 32:8).

There are times when God's will is revealed through a very strong personal desire or dream to accomplish some goal. Those with God-given dreams are also given the determination and divine providence to achieve their desires and fulfill their dreams.

God gives other people special abilities. We sometimes say that God has especially gifted these people in some area of their lives. Some abilities are present nearly from birth and are indicators of God's will for the person's life. Those who possess these gifts and know God have the joy of pursuing the development of these gifts for His glory and will.

God has created you with a divine purpose. Your mission is to let Him gently take you by the hand and guide you to that end, making you more like Him along the way.

Ask yourself this question: *Does God want me to use the talents and gifts He has given me to accomplish great things and glorify His name?* The answer seems obvious, but, sadly, many Christians today are under the false impression that God is automatically opposed to anything they may desire to do if it is not traditional Christian service, such as being a pastor or a missionary. Just because you choose not to sell everything and move to the farthest ends of the earth to live with bugs the size of Volkswagens does not mean you are outside of God's will.

The truth is that many people's deepest desires are legitimate before God. In fact, He can impress things on our hearts and minds that He wants us to do—things He knows we will be good at, because He made us that way. Dr. Harold Sala, a well-known author and radio host, once told me: "Your innermost dreams and heartfelt desires are often the faint outline of God's will for your life."

As you open yourself up to God, an important transformation will begin to take place within your heart and mind as God directs you and shapes your desires according to His will. Your old dreams and desires may become streamlined, changed, or even replaced.

When you live in total abandonment to God, you see the gifts and abilities He has given you in a brand-new light. You will begin to understand that God may use your intellect, physical ability, position in life, education, or natural gifts (in art, science, administration, and so on) to glorify Himself. If you apply yourself to living for Him, you will see how He can divinely guide you into the place He wants you to be and fulfill the desires of your heart in the process.

Be open to God's ways. Beware of insisting on your own way and refusing to submit to the divine will of God. Isaiah 55:9 (NASB) says: "For as the heavens are higher than the earth, so are My ways higher than your ways, and My thoughts than your thoughts." Often we do not fully understand what God is doing, but the key to knowing the will of God and realizing our hearts' desires is to give God the freedom to use our lives as He desires. It's like placing our lives in the palm of His hand. The more we try to push our own agenda on God, the less happy we will be.

I grew up in a musical home. My father, a professional singer, had a deep desire to land a recording contract. When I was growing up, almost every weekend my dad and mom would dress up my sister and me in our Sunday best and take us to Beverly Hills to pass out Dad's demo records to the stars. In those days, you could easily walk right up to the front doors of the homes of Hollywood's biggest names. Often we would meet the celebrities themselves.

One weekend we came to the home of superstar Rock Hudson. We approached his door and knocked. A maid answered and brought us into the foyer of his home. She said, "Mr. Hudson is not home and I do not know when he will return."

My dad was disappointed, but I was ready to jump out of my skin with excitement, because right there in front of me in the foyer was one of the finest drum sets I had ever seen. Since the age of four, I had wanted to play the drums. It was the deepest desire of my heart. However, due to my dad's bad experience in the music industry, he prohibited me from playing any instrument.

Rock Hudson's drums were painted in psychedelic colors, and I could not take my eyes off them. However, I soon noticed something strange. Every single drum skin in the set had been punctured, as if someone had cut each one with a knife.

I asked the maid why the drum set was in such bad condition. She told me that Mr. Hudson would come home late at night, play the drums, and hit them so hard they would puncture. Her words made me so mad. It didn't seem fair. Obviously Mr. Hudson saw the drum set as merely a toy to play with and destroy. I longed to play the drums, and here was a movie star with a drum set that he didn't even care about. No, life didn't seem fair to me at all.

Later, at age twelve, I finally got the opportunity to play an instrument, but it was not the drums. I chose the guitar. Because I had been kept from playing an instrument all those years, my desire and commitment were stronger than ever. I began playing in bands at the age of thirteen and later went abroad to pursue a career in rock 'n' roll. However, as God had planned it, during that pursuit I surrendered my life to Jesus Christ in London. Since then I have been able to play in different settings—both recording and live—all over the world. But now I do it for Christ. You see, what I felt my earthly father meant for harm, my heavenly Father meant for good. God had a better plan than mine—I just needed to be open to His ways.

The Desire of Your Heart

Get alone with God and search your heart in the presence of His Spirit. Be honest and realistic with yourself. Write down the desires of your heart. Pray about them, investigate them, and consider them. At first, you will find that many of the things you desire are not really your ultimate desires after all. Other desires will begin to stand out as priorities. Being thoughtful and prayerful will help you know your Creator better as well as yourself.

King David expressed his heart's cry to the Lord when he said, "I waited patiently for the LORD to help me, and he turned to me and heard my cry" (Ps. 40:1 NLT). In essence this verse is saying, "Don't give up." In time, if you continue seeking the Lord, you will experience the blessing of your desires fulfilled as you accomplish His will.

In the movie *Chariots of Fire*, Eric Liddell consults his pastor concerning the opportunity to compete in the Olympics. His pastor's response is classic: "Eric, you can peel a spud to perfection if you do it in the name of Christ. So run in the name of God!"[6]

When Liddell ran, he ran with abandon. And it wasn't pretty. His arms flapped like a bird, his knees banged awkwardly high, his shoulders bent backward, and his chin pointed straight to the sky. Yet an enormous groundswell of support began rising among the fans for this underdog from Scotland. Suddenly the unorthodox sprinter had become a modern-day hero. However, when Liddell refused to run on

Sunday, eyebrows around the world were raised. Liddell put God first and his running second.

God blessed Liddell's dedication, and the world took notice. Liddell's desire to run, when put in the right priority, brought glory to God.

God wants to bless you and give you the desires of your heart. As you follow His principles of guidance, you will open yourself up to His grand vistas of blessing. And as He did for Eric Liddell, the Lord will use your desires to bring Him glory.

Digging Deeper: Thinking about Your Desires and Dreams

What do you really want in life? What desires has God put in your heart? Take some time to pray about your dreams and desires. Separate those that seem realistic and that you hope to achieve from those that may be unrealistic or that now may not be as important to you or to God as they may have been at one time.

Get out your journal and write down your dreams and desires. Place them in priority from the most urgent to least important. By the way, there is nothing wrong with putting down exact details about the particular desires you have listed.

Pray about how fulfilling your desires can move forward God's kingdom. God wants to fulfill your desires and accomplish His will in the process. This is a very important point. The promises in God's Word concerning your desires are conditioned on His will.

As time goes by and you learn new things about yourself and your desires, revise the list. When certain goals or desires have been achieved or if they change, note the changes and keep praying for God's will in accomplishing them. Remember, times change, and so do we.

Moving from thinking about your dreams to writing them down will help you begin to convert your dreams into actual goals.

One of the wisest things you can do is begin praying daily for your most cherished desires. Never make idols of them, but seek God's will as it relates to them. He will often confirm your desires, cause you to see them in a different light, or change them completely.

The reality of your faith concerning any goal, desire, or dream can be directly related to your preparation for its achievement. God honors your preparation. Clearly, there will be times when all you can do is pray and trust in Him to make your dream a reality. But other times you will be able to specifically prepare for the time ahead when your dreams are fulfilled.

When you put the divine principles contained in God's Word to work for you, which is the express purpose of this book, you will see His will beginning to unfold in an extraordinary way.

"Now glory be to God! By his mighty power at work within us, he is able to accomplish infinitely more than we would ever dare to ask or hope" (Eph. 3:20 NLT).

5

Faith

Finding God's Best

This is a story about a man named Joe who inherited a million dollars. The will, however, provided that Joe had to accept the money either in Chile or Brazil. He chose Brazil. Too bad. It turned out that in Chile, he would have received his inheritance in land on which uranium, gold, and silver had just been discovered. Once in Brazil, Joe had to choose between receiving his inheritance in coffee or nuts. He chose nuts. Again, too bad. The bottom fell out of the nut market and coffee went up to a buck-fifty a pound, wholesale. Poor Joe lost everything he had to his name.

He went out and sold his gold watch for the money he needed to fly back home. It seems that he had just enough for a ticket to New York or Boston. He chose Boston. When the plane for New York taxied up, he noticed it was a brand-new 747 super-

jet with all the latest technology. The plane for Boston arrived and it was a 1928 old Ford tri-motor with a swayback. It was filled with crying children and tethered goats and sheep. It seemed like it took all day to get off the runway. Over the Andes, one of the engines fell off. Our man Joe made his way to the captain and said, "I'm a jinx on this plane. Let me out if you want to save your lives. Give me a parachute." The pilot agreed. "On this plane, anybody who bails out must wear two parachutes," he said. So Joe jumped out of the plane.

As he fell through the air, he tried to make up his mind which rip cord to pull. Finally, he chose the one on the left. It was rusty and the wire pulled loose. So he pulled the other handle. The chute opened, but its shroud line snapped. In desperation, Joe cried out, "Saint Francis, save me!" A hand reached out of heaven and grabbed the poor man by the wrist and let him dangle in midair. Then a gentle but inquisitive voice asked, "Saint Francis Xavier or Saint Francis of Assisi?"

No one knows for sure what happened to poor Joe that day, but we can probably assume that he chose the wrong Saint.[1]

Some of the most difficult, challenging, and exciting times in your life will be when you face important decisions.

Now faith is the substance of things hoped for, the evidence of things not seen.

Hebrews 11:1

WHEN YOU CONSIDER FAITH, what comes to mind?

I've heard people define faith as kind of a fuzzy, unreachable, inner belief that somehow makes things happen.

Certainly faith has to do with your belief in God. But faith is also a practical, hands-on approach to living that makes things happen. Often faith simply operates hand in hand with God as He works out His divine principles in your life.

Faith Exercises

Let's explore five specific exercises of faith that will help you understand how to cooperate with God as He turns your dreams into the reality He desires for you.

1. Turn Dreams into Goals

In the previous chapter you thought about your dreams and desires. I asked you to write them in your journal and to refine them as God gave you insight. Now it's time to turn those dreams into goals—the things you hope to accomplish for God, your family, your church, your community, your world, and yourself.

The history of the founding of the ancient city of Troy illustrates the need to act on your dreams and turn them into goals.

On January 6, 1822, the wife of a poor German pastor had a son, never dreaming he would one day achieve world renown and great wealth. The name of this son was Heinrich Schliemann.

When Heinrich Schliemann was seven years old, a picture of ancient Troy in flames captured his imagination. Contrary to what many people believed, Heinrich argued that Homer's great poems, the *Iliad* and the *Odyssey*, were based on historic facts, and he set out to prove it. In 1873, he uncovered the ancient site of Troy, along with some fabulous treasure, which he smuggled out of the country, much to the anger of the Turkish government.

Schliemann became a famous, wealthy man because he dared to believe an ancient record and act upon his faith.[2]

Schliemann acted on his dream—and so must you!

Like Heinrich Schliemann, who acted on his belief in Homer's great poems and discovered Troy along with great treasure, we must act on the written Word of God to discover His will and the accompanying treasure of His blessings for our lives. Launch out in faith and move forward with the dreams the Lord has given you.

Faith in God's Word sometimes requires us to go against the opinions of others around us. When we have a proper understanding of God's Word combined with a dream from God, we should launch out in faith and ask God to direct us in our endeavors for Him. This is what Abraham did: "By faith Abraham obeyed when he was called to go out to the place which he would afterward receive as an inheritance. And he went out, not knowing where he was going" (Heb. 11:8).

2. *Turn Goals into Plans*

Have you ever noticed that most people have few if any plans for the future? Why? Perhaps because the hectic pace of life crowds out their time for contemplation and planning. With cell phones, pagers, laptops, and the barrage of activity buzzing around us, it's no wonder we have so little time to contemplate, pray, listen for God's voice, and plan the steps our lives will take. Procrastination also takes its toll. We're often like the man who wanted to go on a diet but had no plans. He kept saying, "Monday I will begin." However, Monday came and went each week—with no plans and no follow-through. Plans are essential if you want to accomplish goals.

Jesus Christ knew the Father's plan for His life, had faith in it, and followed it to the end. The purpose and plan of His life was to save the world from sin. He said, "For the Son of Man has come to seek and to save that which was lost" (Luke 19:10).

As the time drew near for His crucifixion, Jesus made steadfast plans to go to Jerusalem. "It came to pass, when the time had come for Him to be received up, that He steadfastly set His face to go to Jerusalem" (9:51). When Christ hung dying on the cross and uttered the words "It is finished!" (John 19:30), He clearly articulated that God's plan was complete.

Indeed, Jesus encourages careful planning when it comes to committing your life to Him: "For which of you, intending to build a tower, does not sit down first and count the cost, whether he has enough to finish it—lest, after he has laid the foundation, and is not able to finish it, all who see it begin to mock him, saying, 'This man began to build and was not able to finish'" (Luke 14:28–30).

Paul the apostle made plans concerning his efforts to reach the church of Asia with the gospel of Christ. He told the church in Corinth: "I was so sure of all this that I made plans to visit you first so you could be blessed twice. I planned to visit you on my way to Macedonia and again on my way back. I wanted to get help from you for my trip to Judea" (2 Cor. 1:15–16 NCV). And he wrote to the Christians in Rome: "Brothers and sisters, I want you to know that I planned many times to come to you, but this has not been possible. I wanted to come so that I could help you grow spiritually as I have helped the other non-Jewish people" (Rom. 1:13 NCV).

What are your plans for the future? What are your specific goals? What do you hope to accomplish in life? How do your current plans fulfill the dreams you may have had for days, months, and even years?

A dictionary definition for the word *plan* provides a great deal of insight at this point. The word *plan* means "to formulate a scheme or program for the accomplishment, enactment, or attainment of a specific goal." When you create a plan, you have a specific aim or purpose.

Consider the person who desires to have a career as a business consultant, with his or her own private practice, and live near the beach. A plan encompassing several steps will be necessary. First, the individual will need to prepare by going to business school. He or she will need to determine the particular type of business on which to concentrate. Will it be management or finance? Will he or she need an advanced degree? Funds will be needed for education. Will he or she work to get through school, borrow from parents, or take out a loan?

Once the person graduates, perhaps he or she will start as an apprentice with a consulting firm that can provide the training and experience needed to ultimately open his or her own practice. For a time, the person may need to sacrifice the goal of living near the beach so that he or she can become well trained. Will the person choose a small firm, providing personal mentors, or a large firm where he or she can learn many specialties under one roof?

Before the new business consultant steps out in faith with his or her own practice, he or she will need to count the cost involved in leasing his or her own office, buying equipment, and paying overhead expenses. Receiving counsel from a successful independent accountant would be extremely beneficial. Living at the beach, of course, will require some research as well. All of these things, and many more, would be required to formulate a plan to accomplish such a goal.

Charting your plan—your destiny—can be exciting and fun. When you devise your plan, be detailed. Write out each major step you must take along the road to success. Personally, I become excited as I mentally chart how I might achieve goals. I love contacting the people who will play a part in making my plans a reality.

By the way, planning will come at different points in our lives. Sometimes it is after we already know the will of God for our lives that we begin to plan. You may have felt driven to a certain goal in life, and after moving toward it, you then began to plan. On the other hand, you may have gone along for some time before realizing that you were unhappy in your present position, and, out of a need to correct your course, you began planning and setting goals to transition to a more fulfilling existence. Of course, there are also those who did not plan to be where they are today but simply got there by the grace of God. God's kingdom is filled with all sorts—so don't be disappointed if you don't fit a certain mold. God has a mold specifically designed for you.

Here's a key point: When you plan, make sure to subject your plans to the will of God. In other words, bring your plans into the shining light of God's Spirit. Submit your goals to God and ask Him to direct you in your planning. Specifically, pray that the Lord will approve or disapprove of your plans through godly counsel, His Word, and providential acts of power.

The Bible speaks directly to this issue. When James addressed certain businessmen in the church, he said:

> Look here, you people who say, "Today or tomorrow we are going to a certain town and will stay there a year. We will do business there and make a profit." How do you know what will happen tomorrow? For your life is like the morning fog—it's here a little while, and it's gone. What you ought to say is, "If the Lord wants us to, we will live and do this or that." Otherwise you will be boasting about your own plans, and all such boasting is evil. Remember, it is sin to know what you ought to do and then not do it.
>
> James 4:13–17 NLT

You should and must plan for the future, but all your planning must be subject to God. God's plans are often different from yours. Be open to divine changes; they are wonderful when they occur.

Proverbs 16:1 says: "People may make plans in their minds, but only the LORD can make them come true" (NCV). You will find that as your plans strike harmony with the will of God for your life, incredible things happen and life becomes all that it was meant to be. "Commit your work to the LORD, and then your plans will succeed" (16:3 NLT).

3. Prepare for Action

It's been said that he who fails to prepare, prepares to fail! Indeed, you are going to find that preparation is one of the most important ingredients in the process of completing your goals. As with so many areas in life, when it comes to preparation, striking a balance is key.

At one end of the spectrum are people who fail to prepare adequately—if at all—for the work involved in making their goals come to fruition. Failure is often the result. However, at the other end of the spectrum are those who prepare endlessly yet never perform. If you are embarking on a never-ending plan of preparation, you may pass up golden opportunities to achieve your goals along the way. You must strike a balance. Normally a certain level of preparation is required to achieve any goal or dream in life. Your specific goals will determine how you prepare for the future.

Education can be a very important part of the process. Are you preparing to go into medicine? Then you will need medical training, which will require you to do research to find the right school. Are you interested in the arts? Maybe you can be an apprentice or attend a school that caters to your specific artistic gifts. Certain goals require education, while others may benefit from special training. Preparation for sports requires athletic training and discipline. Those who want to excel in their field must train diligently.

John Roach Straton had a reputation as a defender of the faith. A young man had come to him and said, "I want to preach." Questioning him, Mr. Straton discovered that he had not finished high school, much less college or seminary. So his advice was to complete all three. The fellow replied, "But I believe that God will fill my mouth." Mr. Straton responded, "Yes, God will fill your mouth if you fill your head first."

Perhaps you are preparing to start a business or planning to retire early so you can concentrate on your real goals. In these instances, your preparation will most likely need to be financial.

What about preparing your family for a cross-country or international move? Any move to a new location requires much preparation—of your home, your belongings, finances, children, pets, and more. Those who have moved realize that preparation can make or break a smooth transition.

It's the same for almost any venture you attempt to tackle in life. *Preparation* is often the key to success. C. S. Lewis expressed it well: "If you give me ten minutes to chop down a tree, I'll spend my first two minutes sharpening my ax."

Whatever your dream is, whatever goals you have set for your life, you must prepare to accomplish them. One of the best ways to begin preparing is with prayer.

In the Old Testament we read of Nehemiah, who was a cupbearer to the king of Persia. When one of his brothers informed him that the walls of Jerusalem were destroyed and that the gates were burned with fire, causing many people to suffer reproach from the neighboring nations, Nehemiah began to fast and pray: "So it was, when I heard these words, that I sat down and wept, and mourned for many days; I was fasting and praying before the God of heaven" (Neh. 1:4).

After some time, Nehemiah requested a leave of absence from the king to go and rebuild the walls and gates of Jerusalem. Not only did the king grant Nehemiah's request, but he also sent him with materials, soldiers, and royal letters of permission. This help from the king made it possible for Nehemiah to successfully complete a desire and burden that God had given him. It all began with prayer.

God is in heaven waiting to answer your petitions just as He did in the life of Nehemiah. Start with prayer and then move forward with your plan!

4. Investigate

Dr. Bill Bright of Campus Crusade for Christ tells this story of a famous oil field called Yates Pool:

> During the depression this field was a sheep ranch owned by a man named Yates. Mr. Yates wasn't able to make enough on his ranching operation to pay the principal and interest on the mortgage, so he was in danger of losing his ranch. With little money for clothes or food, his family (like many others) had to live on government subsidy.
>
> Day after day, as he grazed his sheep over those rolling West Texas hills, he was no doubt greatly troubled about how he would pay his bills. Then a seismographic crew from an oil company came into the area and told him there might be oil on his land. They asked permission to drill a wildcat well, and he signed a lease contract.
>
> At 1,115 feet they struck a huge oil reserve. The first well came in at 80,000 barrels a day. Many subsequent wells were more than twice as large. In fact, 30 years after the discovery, a government test of one of the wells showed it still had the potential flow of 125,000 barrels of oil a day.
>
> And Mr. Yates owned it all. The day he purchased the land he had received the oil and mineral rights. Yet, he'd been living on relief. A multimillionaire living in poverty. The problem? He didn't know the oil was there even though he owned it.
>
> Many Christians live in spiritual poverty. They are entitled to the gifts of the Holy Spirit and his energizing power, but they are not aware of their birthright.[3]

Investigation is another exercise of faith we need to pursue as we seek to fulfill God's plan for our lives. Ephesians 5:17 (NLT) says: "Don't act thoughtlessly, but try to understand what the Lord wants you to do." The word *understand* means "to comprehend and be wise." It also carries with it the idea of examining and investigating something with great care and conveys the concept of being alert. Though this verse primarily refers to the will of God in salvation, it also teaches that God's practical will for our lives can be understood and lived through the process of investigation.

Decisions in life range from choosing the right marriage partner or career to selecting the best investment opportunity or location in which to live. Indeed, some decisions are of life-and-death proportions. Most major decisions require investigation, and many people are suffering today because they passed by this essential step.

Jesus gave us a key to investigation when He taught, "Ask, and it will be given to you; seek, and you will find; knock, and it will be opened to you" (Matt. 7:7). If you hope to accomplish goals and realize the will of God in your life, you will need to ask God for guidance as you seek solutions to life's predicaments. A more contemporary reading of this verse is enlightening: "Keep on asking, and you will be given what you ask for. Keep on looking, and you will find. Keep on knocking, and the door will be opened" (NLT).

When the Israelites reached the land God had promised them, Moses sent out twelve spies to investigate. Likewise, Joshua, before attempting to conquer Jericho, sent out two reconnaissance spies. And Nehemiah surveyed the rubble and burned-down walls of Jerusalem before he began rebuilding.

As you work your way through your decisions in life and seek to accomplish your goals, you will need to do constant investigation. Faith means that you continue to move forward, always looking for the perfect place where your way and God's way meet. When you do, you will come to His desired purpose, because He reveals His will as we act in faith.

Are you acting in faith today? Have you given your dreams, goals, and ambitions completely to God? He is calling you and wants to walk hand in hand with you, showing you the way.

Life is a grand treasure hunt with many blessings in store when you investigate your options, look to God for direction, and accomplish the goals He has set for you.

5. Seek Godly Counsel

"Where there is no counsel, the people fall; but in the multitude of counselors there is safety" (Prov. 11:14). Without question, counsel is one of the most important facets of learning to walk by faith. Counsel is also one of the most neglected and lost arts of our time. In biblical times, the wise and elderly men and women in each community were the leaders, mentors, and counselors of their day. Unfortunately, our society has lost sight of this vital resource. We've relegated our older and wiser people to live in retirement, while many of us, struggling along on our own, fail miserably because we don't take advantage of their valuable counsel.

There are literally hundreds of verses in the Bible on counsel. Here are just a few:

- "You will guide me with Your counsel, and afterward receive me to glory" (Ps. 73:24).
- "Listen to counsel and receive instruction, that you may be wise in your latter days" (Prov. 19:20).
- "There are many plans in a man's heart, nevertheless the LORD's counsel—that will stand" (v. 21).
- "Counsel in the heart of man is like deep water, but a man of understanding will draw it out" (20:5).
- "Plans are established by counsel; by wise counsel wage war" (v. 18).
- "This also comes from the LORD of hosts, who is wonderful in counsel and excellent in guidance" (Isa. 28:29).

Counsel from trusted, godly friends will help shape your destiny for God. You may be surprised when you receive input from trusted friends. Sometimes the input will confirm your desires, and at other times it will challenge and contradict your thoughts.

Make sure to choose counselors who are wise and godly and who have your best interests at heart. A person who counsels you in any matter should be focused on what is best for you. This person should have integrity, spiritual depth, and a strong life experience—including failure. Young, qualified counselors are rare. Good counselors are often older and mature. Consider your friends, family, and some acquaintances as potential counselors who might be able to guide you in specific areas of your life.

At different times in your life, you will need counsel from different people. When you need help with relationship decisions, you will want to seek advice from people who have been successful in relationships, such as a happily married man or woman or a parent who has raised solid children who are mentally and spiritually whole. At other times, an excellent source of wisdom may be a professional in his or her field, such as a doctor, lawyer, educator. A respected tradesperson, such as a carpenter, or a highly esteemed athletic coach could also be an excellent source of wisdom. The counselors you rely on should be well experienced, possibly having already gone through midlife and career changes.

Harvey Penick was the golf coach at the University of Texas from 1931 to 1963 and the golf mentor for some of the greats: Ben Crenshaw, Tom Kite, Kathy Whitworth, Betsy Rawls, and Mickey Wright. They returned to Penick even after years on the pro golfers' circuit to seek his help with their putting, chipping and driving.

Like any good coach, Penick was a careful observer who learned how to golf from watching others. In fact, for decades Penick scribbled his random observations about golf into a notebook. One day he mentioned these golf diaries to a writer named Bud Shrake. Shrake saw the publishing potential in Penick's notebooks and collaborated with him on a book published in 1992 under the title *Harvey Penick's Little Red Book: Lessons and Teachings from a Lifetime in Golf*. The *Little Red Book* sold more than a million copies, becoming the best-selling sports book in history. Penick was eighty-seven years old.

Most older people haven't written a *Little Red Book*, but like Penick observing golfers, they've observed life and learned important things the hard way. A wise person takes seriously the wisdom of older people.[4]

Remember that the source of all good and true counsel is ultimately God. He is the fountain from which all great counsel flows. An Old Testament proverb says it best:

All who fear the LORD will hate evil. That is why I hate pride, arrogance, corruption, and perverted speech. Good advice and success belong to me. Insight and strength are mine. Because of me, kings reign, and rulers make just laws. Rulers lead with my help, and nobles make righteous judgments.

I love all who love me. Those who search for me will surely find me.

Proverbs 8:13–17 NLT

God's School of Faith

I would imagine if God had a university, the motto etched in stone over the entrance would read: "God's School of Faith—Where We Build Faith the Old-Fashioned Way, We Test It!"

God's school of faith is like no other school on earth. God Himself must enroll you, and He is the One who permits you to graduate when you are finished. His curriculum is tailor-made for you because only He—the Creator—knows your makeup. As God puts you through these periods of training, He calls you simply to obey and stand strong as He works out His divine plan to build your faith.

If you are like me, you will try to avoid the school of faith at all costs. But you can be sure of one thing: Before God uses you for any great task, He will put you through His faith-building training program. Each faith-building program differs in certain respects, but the end result is always the same—increased faith in God.

> Remember how the LORD your God has led you in the desert for these forty years, taking away your pride and testing you, because he wanted to know what was in your heart. He wanted to know if you would obey his commands. He took away your pride when he let you get hungry, and then he fed you with manna, which neither you nor your ancestors had ever seen. This was to teach you that a person does not live by eating only bread, but by everything the LORD says.
>
> Deuteronomy 8:2–3 NCV

You see, God is in the business of preparing us in His school of faith to do great things for Him, just as He prepared Israel for their conquest and possession of the Promised Land. It is wonderful to consider that despite almost impossible odds against this tiny nation, today, thousands of years later, it again possesses that same land.

Today God is training you for His glory. Therefore take heart and understand that He is working all things for good in your life. This should give you hope so that you can benefit from God's school of faith, even when it seems that His program is tough!

Tests of Time

Moses spent forty years in the desert training for one of the greatest faith assignments ever undertaken—to lead the slave nation Israel out from beneath the iron-fisted grip of Egypt. Though Moses had been prepared in the universities of Egypt, God's training ground was quite different. After failing miserably to rescue even one Israelite from the hand of an Egyptian taskmaster, Moses fled to Midian, a nowhere town in the desert. Then for forty years he learned the *real* lessons of life. Moses attended the Desert University of God and received a bachelor's degree in faith.

One of the greatest and most profitable lessons Moses learned was that he could do *nothing* without God.

Perhaps you feel you are in some forgotten outpost. But remember, the Lord has not forgotten you. It may be that at this very moment, He is preparing you for the ultimate work of your lifetime.

Take heart, God is building your faith. Don't jump to conclusions and assume you are undergoing some kind of pass-or-fail test. No. You are in a proving ground where God refines you and prepares you to accept His will. God will test your heart to prepare you for the work He has for you to do.

First Peter 1:6–7 says: "In this you greatly rejoice, though now for a little while, if need be, you have been grieved by various trials, that the genuineness of your faith, being much more precious than gold that perishes, though it is tested by fire, may be found to praise, honor, and glory at the revelation of Jesus Christ." The Greek word for *tested* here is the word used for those who test metals (assayers). The literal meaning is "to approve, allow, discern, examine, and try." God performs tests and purifies in extraordinary ways.

Consider the story of how gold is refined.

The assayer of gold takes the raw pieces of gold fresh from the mountain dig and places them in a pot and slides the pot into a fiery hot furnace. Once the gold is melted, he then removes the pot from the furnace for the first wave of purification. The impure elements that were not real gold float to the top. He then skims the impurities, called dross, off the top of the gold and slides the pot back into the furnace once again. This exercise of skimming dross and placing the pot back in the fire occurs over and over until finally the dross is totally removed and the gold is pure.

How did the assayer know when the dross was completely removed and the gold was pure? When he looked into the pot full of molten gold, he could see his reflection as in a mirror shining in the gold itself.

So too God puts your heart to the test to prepare you for His will, and He knows when you are ready. That's when He looks into your face and can see Christ's reflection in you. "The refining pot is for silver and the furnace for gold, but the LORD tests the hearts" (Prov. 17:3).

Tests of the Will

His name was Lt. John Blanchard, a soldier in basic training in Florida during WW II. One evening he wandered into the post library and found a book to read. The feminine handwriting in the margins intrigued him, so he turned to the front of the book and found the name of the previous owner . . . a Miss Hollis Maynell.

Blanchard did some research and found her address in New York. The following day he was shipped overseas. For thirteen months the two corresponded by letter and began to open their hearts to each other. He asked for her picture, to which she refused by saying that if he really loved her it wouldn't matter what she looked like.

Finally the day came when they were to meet in Grand Central Station, New York City. She had instructed, "You'll recognize me by the red rose that I'll be wearing on my lapel."

Let's let the young soldier tell you what happened:

"A young woman was coming toward me, beautiful, trim, blonde, eyes were blue as flowers, and in her pale green suit she was like springtime come alive. I started toward her forgetting that she was not wearing the rose . . . and then I saw Hollis Maynell.

"She was standing behind the girl. A woman with graying hair. But, she wore a red rose on the rumpled brown lapel of her coat. So deep was my longing for the woman whose spirit had captured me that I approached her. There she stood. Her face was gentle and sensible and her gray eyes had a twinkle. I didn't hesitate. My hand gripped the small worn blue leather book, which was to identify me to her.

"I squared my shoulders and saluted and held out the book to the woman even while choking back the bitterness of disappointment. 'I'm Lt. John Blanchard and you must be Miss Maynell. I am so glad to meet you. May I take you to dinner?' The woman's face broadened into a smile.

"'I don't know what this is about, son,' she answered, 'but the young lady in the green suit who just went by asked me to wear this rose. And she said if you were to ask me out to dinner I should tell you that she is waiting for you in the large restaurant across the street. She said it was some kind of test!'"

Apparently, Lt. John Blanchard passed the test. Would you?[5]

Your tests may come in a variety of ways and means. They may come as a challenge to forgive; a challenge to accept things you would otherwise reject (as in the case of Lt. John Blanchard); a challenge to survive during persecution, sickness, or hardship; or a challenge to muster up confidence in the face of failure. Often God tests by asking you to surrender something you cherish that is competing for your worship of Him. Remember that you can worship only one thing at a time—make sure it is God, always God.

"God, examine me and know my heart; test me and know my nervous thoughts. See if there is any bad thing in me. Lead me on the road to everlasting life" (Ps. 139:23–24 NCV).

Tests of Trials

In any great venture, obstacles will come. At these times, God will help you persevere and overcome the things that stand in your way. I urge you to treat obstacles as invited guests, because God is working in them and through them for your good, building your faith in extraordinary ways.

The Old Testament patriarch Isaac gives us beautiful direction in this area. Isaac had become quite wealthy, and his flocks and servants grew in number. Because he was in the foreign land of Canaan (the Promised Land was still a distant promise), he needed somewhere to settle. His plight gives great insight into this component of faith that is so necessary to exercise in our daily lives. Let's permit God's Word to tell the story:

> [Isaac] became a rich man, and his wealth only continued to grow. He acquired large flocks of sheep and goats, great herds of cattle, and many servants. Soon the Philistines became jealous of him, and they filled up all of Isaac's wells with earth. These were the wells that had been dug by the servants of his father, Abraham.
>
> And Abimelech asked Isaac to leave the country. "Go somewhere else," he said, "for you have become too rich and powerful for us."
>
> So Isaac moved to the Gerar Valley and lived there instead. He reopened the wells his father had dug, which the Philistines had filled in after Abraham's death. Isaac renamed them, using the names Abraham had given them. His shepherds also dug in the Gerar Valley and found a gushing spring.
>
> But then the local shepherds came and claimed the spring. "This is our water," they said, and they argued over it with Isaac's herdsmen. So Isaac named the well "Argument," because they had argued about it with him. Isaac's men then dug another well, but again there was a fight over it. So Isaac named it "Opposition." Abandoning that one, he dug another well, and the local people finally left him alone. So Isaac called it "Room Enough," for he said, "At last the LORD has made room for us, and we will be able to thrive."
>
> Genesis 26:13–22 NLT

Isaac's hardship is relevant in your life today. Why? Because it teaches that when you encounter opposition, the key is to persevere until the Lord gives you peace and rest in the land, just as He did with Isaac.

What is the name of the well you are digging today? Is it Opposition or Argument? I urge you to keep on digging and searching, because you will come to "Room Enough," and God will confirm His will to you in a wonderful way.

Don't be afraid of the testing process. If you are close to God, He will bring you success and bless you through His works and gifts. If you place your complete trust and confidence in Him, you can expect Him to guide you into His will.

God has a personal training program for you, and I hope you are ready to participate in it so that you can say with Job, "God knows the way that I take, and when he has tested me, I will come out like gold" (Job 23:10 NCV).

How Much Faith Do You Have?

Your faith must be active for you to realize the potential God has for you. As I have observed faith in the lives of others and myself, I have found that the greatest obstacle of faith is fear.

Recently I was watching my six-year-old son, Christopher, play in a championship soccer match. Soccer at that age is exciting, because the kids are just maturing physically, and they are trying with their little growing bodies to defend the goal, kick the ball, and score. A motley crew of boys surrounded the ball and fought to boot it. Dust flew as they pushed, kicked, and flopped to the ground. The cluster of boys moved downfield in a blaze of fury. Meanwhile, the parents were yelling and screaming at the top of their lungs: "Go, number 10!" "Take it away from him, Johnny!" "Score, Blue!" "Go, Red!" It was one of those experiences that assaults the senses.

As I watched these little guys, I noticed something about each player that inspired me concerning how we do or do not act in faith. As the game went on, I separated the kids into three types of players. Each typified a different level of faith. As you read about the three groups below, you will likely associate yourself with one of the three levels of faith, whether it describes your faith as it relates to a certain goal in life or to life itself.

Little Fearful

During the game, several boys meandered on the outskirts of the action. They were not among the pack of boys who were going after the ball but were watching from a distance. Some even turned away from the game and looked toward their parents or toward something else that caught their attention. The coach would repeatedly call their names to get them to participate, but eventually he just gave up and focused his attention on those who gave him the hope of winning. As I studied these boys, I realized that fear was paralyzing them and keeping them from helping the team defend their goal and score points.

There are many people who are fearful when it comes to accomplishing life's goals. When it is time to take serious action, they end up just standing and looking on. Golden opportunities arise and they excuse themselves, saying something like, "Oh, I cannot possibly do that." "I'm too young." "I'm too old." "I'm not good enough." "I'm not prepared." Often they withdraw from the opportunity altogether.

We must get over our fear if we are going to do anything worthwhile in life. Like the soccer coach who was trying to get the kids involved, God is calling you to action, but because of your fear, you may have learned to ignore His voice.

How do you conquer your fear? Put your full trust in Christ, not in yourself.

The apostle Peter once watched Jesus walk on water. Known for his outspokenness, even pushiness, Peter said spontaneously,

> "Lord, if it's really you, tell me to come to you by walking on water."
> "All right, come," Jesus said.
> So Peter went over the side of the boat and walked on the water toward Jesus. But when he looked around at the high waves, he was terrified and began to sink. "Save me, Lord!" he shouted.

Instantly Jesus reached out his hand and grabbed him. "You don't have much faith," Jesus said. "Why did you doubt me?"

Matthew 14:28–31 NLT

This is such a wonderful illustration of the way we often fail because of fear. It shows that the key to overcoming fear is keeping your eyes on Jesus, not on yourself, not on your circumstances. Paul the apostle said it best: "We learned not to rely on ourselves, but on God who can raise the dead" (2 Cor. 1:9 NLT). "For I can do everything with the help of Christ who gives me the strength I need" (Phil. 4:13 NLT).

Very Cautious

Another group of boys in the soccer match seemed engaged in the game as they ran to and fro, but they were visibly cautious. They would run up and down the field, close to the circle of boys fighting to move the ball, but they rarely joined in the fray. All the while, the coach was turning red as he yelled at them, "Get in there, number 7! Kick that ball; fight for it! Come on, 3, get in there!" By the end of the game, those little players on the outskirts were exhausted, even though they had not been productive.

There are people who exchange their dreams and goals for a cautious and comfortable lifestyle. Some run through each day too busy to stop and consider what God may want to do in their lives. Others tag along with the successful people around them and admire their lives but take no initiative to accomplish their own goals. Some excuse themselves by saying they are analyzing things and waiting for the best opportunity, but it never comes. Indeed, caution can be a mask for fear, and sometimes simple laziness is the problem.

There comes a time when we must stop making excuses and looking inward at our fears and look to Christ instead. At some point, we must step out in faith. A wise, older man once said to me: "Gary, do you know the difference between a rut and a grave? A rut is a grave with the ends knocked out."

Solomon, the great king of Israel, wrote: "He who observes the wind will not sow, and he who regards the clouds will not reap" (Eccles. 11:4). The New Living Translation puts it this way: "If you wait for perfect conditions, you will never get anything done."

God is calling you who are cautious today, saying: "Get in there and play; fight for that ball. I have a wonderful plan for your life. Determine the root of your caution and conquer it. And remember this: One of the greatest failures in decision making is the refusal to decide."

Great Faith

Finally, there was a circle of boys who were caught up in the middle of the action. They were moving the ball constantly toward the goal, kicking, passing, running, screaming, and falling. What a great experience it was to watch these little ones! I was virtually swept away with their action. The coach loved them because they listened and were attentive—and they scored. They were sweaty, tired, and happy because they were using their skills to do what they desired.

The boys who were successful and scored had four things in common:

1. knowledge of the game
2. an observable goal
3. a plan to achieve that goal
4. faith in their ability to play

God has given you those same qualities:

1. knowledge of the game of life found in the Word of God
2. observable goals that proceed from realizing God's will for your life

3. a plan that arises from the principles of knowing the will of God for your life
4. faith in God in spite of your own inabilities and flaws

God has fantastic plans for your life, but because of many human factors such as fear, unbelief, laziness, or an unconsecrated life, you can miss all the blessed things that He has planned for you.

Faith and God's Will

When you have faith, you will also have times of searching—times when God clearly bids you to step out to determine His will in a matter. This can come in the area of courtship for marriage, new direction for your career, finding a home, or even a cure for illness. Often as the search begins, you will have a particular idea of what the desired outcome will be, but you will discover that the results are even better than you had imagined. Sometimes God allows the time to be extended when you must wait on Him. In these instances, you must learn to wait patiently, trusting that God, in His timing, will bring to pass the desired results.

No matter what your situation, as you faithfully walk with God, He will lead. He will direct you providentially into situations, settings, and circumstances that will help you. And, as God leads, you will find that the desires of your heart are being molded and shaped into His desires—and His will.

When you commit your future to God, not only will He use your existing talents and desires; He will give you new spiritual gifts (see Rom. 12:6–8; 1 Cor. 12:1–10; Eph. 4:11–12) and may even direct you in a whole new way. You will be happy when you are fulfilling God's purpose.

Through faith you will confidently conclude: This is the will of God for my life!

God has given you incredible wisdom from His Word, coupled with the mental faculties to know and determine His best choices for you. You are to put them to use and make the right decisions. The following is a bit of verse I wrote that describes the life lived by faith:

> Our lives wind through many miles,
> across rivers, through icy snow,
> dark and bleak nights and cloudy days,
> through intense storms where we learn
> to trust in Him and grow.
> Long, hot, and arid deserts where
> we learn to abandon our own self-trust
> and lay down our lives for His sake
> to live for that which is just.
> But it is in these moments
> that we grow close to Him.
> He is always there for us,
> yet the end of the journey is always predictable . . .
> Breathless beauty, the sun-filled sky,
> awesome streams flow where God bids we go.
> The joy of salvation,
> the comfort of love,
> patience of heart,
> and power from above,
> these are the things that God
> has willed and yet there is more
> that He has still.
> For we travel an appointed way.

"Now glory be to God! By his mighty power at work within us, he is able to accomplish infinitely more than we would ever dare to ask or hope. May he be given glory in the church and in Christ Jesus forever and ever through endless ages. Amen" (Eph. 3:20–21 NLT).

Digging Deeper: Practical Tips to Increase Your Faith

Finding the will of God is in some ways like a grand search throughout life. Perhaps this is because we often try to achieve our goals, complete our plans, and do our thing without first giving ourselves to Him. This can result in major failures and discouragement.

Take the journal in which you have listed your goals, dreams, and desires—and set a strategy. Your strategy should include a plan, which you will need to investigate.

Once you have prayed about a certain life direction, it will be important to begin testing the waters in that direction as you attempt to see where the Lord may lead you. There is nothing wrong with stepping out in faith and trying various ventures, until you find what you believe is your heart's desire and God's divine will.

Keeping in mind the principles of faith we have covered thus far, ask yourself these questions:

- Am I being patient through the process?
- Does God have me in a holding pattern right now? (If so, be patient.)
- Have certain obstacles come up that require me to persevere or possibly change direction?
- Am I being tested? If so, I must remember that I am also being refined like gold.

Faith is not simply a blank check from God so that you can have anything you desire. Rather, faith is a privilege you've been given to receive all of those things God desires you to have for the furtherance of His love on earth. When you pursue God's will for your life, you must do so believing Him, His Word, and His ways. "For nothing is impossible with God" (Luke 1:37 NLT).

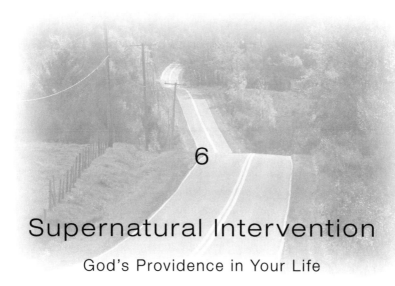

6

Supernatural Intervention

God's Providence in Your Life

*On June 8, 1972, U.S. Army Staff Officer John Plummer was
called upon to provide air support for allied troops in a small
Vietnamese village. Plummer was told that there were no
civilians in the village, but the next day, he learned otherwise.
In a military newspaper, he saw a photo of two children
running down the road, screaming and crying. One of them, a
nine-year-old girl, named Kim Phuc, was naked. Her clothing
had been burned off her body by the jellied gasoline that had
been dropped the day before. Plummer was absolutely
devastated.*

*One picture they say is worth a thousand words. In this case,
it was worth a thousand nightmares. Though Plummer tried
to suppress the image, he couldn't. It devastated his life. Anne
Gearan, writing for the Associated Press, said, "For decades,*

Plummer struggled with his conscience. He drank and divorced. He searched for God." And then God found him. In 1990 John Plummer was converted to Jesus Christ and found God's forgiveness. He said, "I realized I did not have to bear the guilt of my sins and all the hurt I caused other people." He soon gave up his job and became a Methodist pastor.

God had been working on the other side of that photo as well. Kim Phuc recovered from the trauma of her experience. Eventually, she, too, became a Christian. The scream that the photo so graphically portrayed became a smile. She married and moved to Canada. In the fall of 1996, Kim spoke at a gathering in Washington, D.C., that John Plummer attended. Following her message, the two met for the first time. When Plummer stepped forward and said, "I'm so sorry," Kim didn't hesitate. She immediately said, "It's all right. I forgive."

For two hours they talked and cried together, and gradually God began the healing process, which only He could perform. The following Sunday, Plummer faced his congregation and told his story. His congregation wept with him.[1]

God is in control of our lives, and He can demonstrate that fact in supernatural ways. These supernatural interventions of God can best be summed up as "providence."

That the world may know that You have sent Me.

John 17:23

THE ENGLISH WORD *providence* means "God guiding human destiny." Providence is God's omniscient direction of the universe and the affairs of humankind with wise benevolence. Providence means God is in control of all things—at all times—and guides our lives with His loving hands.

God's providence is comforting. It assures us that He loves us and has great plans in store for us. Simply stated, this means that every one of God's miracles has a specific purpose. They are not mere wonders or exhibitions of power just to excite and amaze. God demonstrates His miraculous power *to reveal Himself to a fallen world*. It is by a miracle that God gave us both His special verbal revelation—the Bible—and His supreme visual revelation—the gift of His own Son, Jesus Christ.[2]

God's providential works did not stop with Christ's coming. They continue today in amazing ways to bring people to the knowledge of God, to glorify Jesus Christ, and to save souls, change lives, and comfort the needy. The following story demonstrates how God uses providence to accomplish His plans for our future in the most extraordinary ways imaginable.

My heart's desire was for a shiny, perfect, purple bicycle, but God had it in His heart to use that longing to give me much, much more. . . .

I had walked past that storefront window countless times. There it was—a shiny, purple, and perfect new bicycle.

There are just some things that all children want, and I was no exception. "Oh, the things I could do with that beautiful new bike!" I thought.

My father was a pastor, and our family did not have a lot of money, so I decided to save my allowance and odd-job money to buy myself the bicycle. Every week I walked past the store to see "my" beautiful purple bike.

I worked hard to save my money and kept praying that God would bring me what I wanted.

One day during Sunday school, my teacher talked about a missionary family in need. She told us about the horrible sickness this family was enduring. Reading from a letter written by the family, she told the class about the little boy who had contracted hepatitis, most likely from a typhoid shot he had received in Chile. All week I thought about the little boy far away in Chile.

The next Sunday my teacher asked us what we should do to help this little boy. All the children decided he could really use a brand new bike—that would cheer him up for sure!

I remember my heart almost stopping: I said, "Oh no, God, not my bike!" But then I knew I had to give my bike money to my teacher so it could help that little boy in Chile get a bike.

One week later, I gave my money to the teacher.

Many years later in college, I began praying that God would send me a godly husband.

My father was still a pastor and was also teaching at a local Baptist college. When I went home for Christmas vacation one year, I met Philip at my father's church. Philip was attending the Baptist college where my father taught. In fact, he was in his class.

Not long after my Christmas break, I decided to transfer to this same college. I got to know Philip better since my college roommate was engaged to his best friend and my parents and Philip's parents were also friends.

Our first date was on Valentine's Day. It soon became obvious that we were made for each other. We decided to get married. I didn't know then just how God-ordained our relationship was.

One evening, after both our families had eaten dinner together, Philip's mom started reminiscing about their missionary days and what life was like on the field with small children. She shared about a time in Chile when the whole family had been terribly sick and how Philip had come down with hepatitis, presumably from a typhoid shot. I couldn't believe what I was hearing! My husband was the little boy that I had given up my bike money for! I had to leave the room because I was so emotional—I just could not stop crying.

God had been so good to me. My heart's desire was for a shiny, perfect, purple bicycle, but God had it in His heart to use that longing to give me much, much more—a godly husband that He had ordained from the very beginning.

Philip and I now have three grown children and have been married for twenty-nine years. We know in our hearts and hold on to the fact that God made us for each other and planned it that way before even time began.[3]

Psalm 32:8 says: "I will guide you along the best pathway for your life. I will advise you and watch over you" (NLT). Our infinite God works in ways that are wonderful to behold. Let us learn some of the providential means by which God has worked in Scripture that we might know Him better and be encouraged.

Past, Present, and Future—God Is at Work

Past

Many of God's providential acts are noticed only after they have passed. We often look back and say, "Wow, God was really guiding me during those, times and I never even knew it." We understand later that God has been gently guiding us through the winding roads of life.

The life of the Old Testament patriarch Joseph is an excellent example.

At seventeen, Joseph was the apple of his father, Jacob's, eye—and was the envy of his ten brothers. God had graced Joseph with dreams about the future. The dreams indicated that he would one day be a ruler and that his parents and brothers would bow down to him. Being young and naive, Joseph told his dreams to his family, which incited his brothers to anger and hatred.

One day the brothers conspired against Joseph and decided to murder him. They threw him into an abandoned well. However, seeing some Midianite slave traders journeying by, they had another thought—they decided to sell him to the Ishmaelite slave traders.

Once in Egypt, the Ishmaelites sold Joseph to a man named Potiphar who was a soldier in the Egyptian guard under Pharaoh. Joseph served Potiphar well and was promoted to a high position, which he held until Potiphar's wayward wife noticed him. She begged him to sleep with her, but he ran out of the house, leaving his torn sleeve in the woman's hand. She screamed, called the guards, and lied that Joseph had attempted to sleep with her. When her husband heard about it, he threw Joseph into prison.

What a horrible set of circumstances befell this young man—betrayed by his very brothers, separated from his father, and sold into slavery in a foreign land! Then, just as his life had begun to take a turn for the better through a promotion, he was falsely accused by his master's wife and condemned to a dungeon for years.

God was preparing Joseph for something great. But first, God's custom character-building shop would do some work in the heart and mind of young Joseph. God's tool for this work would not be a mighty university or the plush home of a king—but a prison cell. Psalm 105:18–19 says: "There in prison, they bruised his feet with fetters and placed his neck in an iron collar until the time came to fulfill his word, the LORD tested Joseph's character" (NLT).

Even in prison, Joseph was eventually promoted to overseer. He served there many years, until one day a plot to kill Pharaoh was unveiled. Two of the king's staff, the chief butler and chief baker, were placed in prison under Joseph's authority. One night both the butler and the baker had strange dreams, and in the morning they sought someone who could interpret the visions. Guess who had the interpretations? Yes, Joseph.

Three days later the baker was put to death and the butler was restored to his position before Pharaoh, exactly as Joseph had predicted. As the butler was about to be released from prison and restored to the king, Joseph pleaded with the butler to remember him and get him out of prison; but, like a fair-weather friend, the butler forgot Joseph. So Joseph remained in prison two more years.

But then something extraordinary happened. Pharaoh was frustrated about one of his own dreams, which no one could interpret. And God used the king's frustration to bring about His divine will for Joseph.

"Then the chief butler spoke to Pharaoh, saying: 'I remember my faults this day. When Pharaoh was angry with his servants, and put me in custody in the house of the captain of the guard, both me and the chief baker, we each dreamed a dream in one night. . . . Now there was a young Hebrew man with us there, a servant of the captain of the guard. And we told him, and he interpreted our dreams for us'" (Gen. 41:9–12).

So Pharaoh called Joseph out of the prison and asked that he interpret his dream, and he did, giving God all the glory for the interpretation.

"Then Pharaoh said to Joseph, 'Inasmuch as God has shown you all this, there is no one as discerning and wise as you. You shall be over my house, and all my people shall be ruled according to your word; only in regard to the throne will I be greater than you'" (vv. 39–41). Joseph went from years of slavery and imprisonment to being second in charge of the greatest nation on earth! But God had even more blessings in store for Joseph. His new position would be used to shelter and save the nation of Israel during a time of worldwide famine.

In time his father, Jacob, would send the very brothers who betrayed Joseph to Egypt to collect grain during the time of famine. When Joseph revealed himself to his brothers, they were terrified, thinking he would kill them all for their betrayal. But here's the key—Joseph comforted them by *pointing out the hand of God in directing the whole tragic situation to a grand destination.* Joseph said, "God sent me before you to preserve a posterity for you in the earth, and to save your lives by a great deliverance. So now it was not you who sent me here, but God" (45:7–8).

Looking back at his life, Joseph could see how God had worked and moved in his dire circumstances to bring about a glorious ending. But he saw it only as he looked back on the situation, not while he was in the midst of it.

Maybe you are in the midst of a difficult situation right now and you don't see God's guidance or divine intervention. Learn a lesson from Joseph and trust God to work for good in your life. In time you will be able to look back at this period and see what He was doing to bring about His glorious will.

Present

God's providential acts can be seen daily through His divine guidance. One of the most incredible biblical examples of God's present guidance comes from the Old Testament account of Abraham, when he was seeking a bride for his son Isaac. The story can help you better understand God's present guidance in your life—and bring you hope.

Abraham wanted to arrange a marriage for his son Isaac. In that day and culture, the parents arranged marriages. Not wanting his son to marry a Canaanite, Abraham sent his servant to Haran to find a bride for Isaac. Genesis tells the story.

> Now Abraham was old, well advanced in age; and the LORD had blessed Abraham in all things. So Abraham said to the oldest servant of his house, who ruled over all that he had, "Please, put your hand under my thigh, and I will make you swear by the LORD, the God of heaven and the God of the earth, that you will not take a wife for my son from the daughters of the Canaanites, among whom I dwell; but you shall go to my country and to my kindred, and take a wife for my son Isaac."
>
> And the servant said to him, "Perhaps the woman will not be willing to follow me to this land. Must I take your son back to the land from which you came?"

But Abraham said to him, "Beware that you do not take my son back there. The LORD God of heaven, who took me from my father's house and from the land of my family, and who spoke to me and swore to me, saying, 'To your descendants I give this land,' He will send His angel before you, and you shall take a wife for my son from there. And if the woman is not willing to follow you, then you will be released from this oath; only do not take my son back there."

So the servant put his hand under the thigh of Abraham his master, and swore to him concerning this matter.

Genesis 24:1–9

The servant had a difficult task and an enormous responsibility. As he approached the city of Haran, where he was to find a bride, he prayed these words:

O LORD God of my master Abraham, please give me success this day, and show kindness to my master Abraham. Behold, here I stand by the well of water, and the daughters of the men of the city are coming out to draw water. Now let it be that the young woman to whom I say, "Please let down your pitcher that I may drink," and she says, "Drink, and I will also give your camels a drink"—let her be the one whom You have appointed for Your servant Isaac. And by this I will know that You have shown kindness to my master.

Verses 12–14

While the servant was still praying, God was working on his behalf!

And it happened, before he had finished speaking, that behold, Rebekah, who was born to Bethuel, son of Milcah, the wife of Nahor, Abraham's brother, came out with her pitcher on her shoulder. Now the young woman was very beautiful to behold, a virgin; no man had known her. And she went down to the well, filled her pitcher, and came up. And the servant ran to meet her and said, "Please let me

115

drink a little water from your pitcher." So she said, "Drink, my lord." Then she hastened and let her pitcher down to her hand, and gave him a drink. And when she had finished giving him a drink, she said, "I will draw water for your camels also, until they have finished drinking."

Verses 15–19

Not only did this young woman water the camels, but she also turned out to be Abraham's relative. The servant praised God for His answer. The key to God's present guidance is found in the servant's response to this miracle: "Blessed be the LORD God of my master Abraham, who has not forsaken His mercy and His truth toward my master. As for me, being on the way, the LORD led me to the house of my master's brethren" (v. 27).

Did you catch the servant's words? "As for me, being on the way, the LORD led me." Yes, God leads us to His appointed destiny. This should inspire great hope in us today. God guides us providentially as we move forward in faith and live for Him while prayerfully seeking His will.

Future

God may give you a glimpse of your life's future direction, though it is far more common to experience God's *present* guidance or recognize His *past* guidance, as in the cases we have already studied.

We should remain sober-minded about any future guidance we may claim to receive from God. Until we look back at our life and at the years that have gone by, we can be certain only that God is, in fact, guiding us to His appointed destiny.

The stunning meeting on the Damascus road between Saul of Tarsus (Paul the apostle) with the risen Christ reveals that God gave this man a glimpse into his future. Paul recounts the history of his conversion in Acts 26:12–18 in a formal hearing before King Agrippa as a defense against the Jewish leaders in Jerusalem who were responsible for his continued imprisonment.

> One day I was on such a mission to Damascus, armed with the authority and commission of the leading priests. About noon, Your Majesty, a light from heaven brighter than the sun shone down on me and my companions. We all fell down, and I heard a voice saying to me in Aramaic, "Saul, Saul, why are you persecuting me? It is hard for you to fight against my will."
>
> "Who are you, sir?" I asked.
>
> And the Lord replied, "I am Jesus, the one you are persecuting. Now stand up! For I have appeared to you to appoint you as my servant and my witness. You are to tell the world about this experience and about other times I will appear to you. And I will protect you from both your own people and the Gentiles. Yes, I am going to send you to the Gentiles, to open their eyes so they may turn from darkness to light, and from the power of Satan to God. Then they will receive forgiveness for their sins and be given a place among God's people, who are set apart by faith in me" (NLT).

In this experience, Christ spoke to Saul and told him about his future as an apostle to the Gentile nations. Clearly this is a rare example of how God works. It is more common for Him to intervene through another person, for example, who gives us insight into God's work for our future. God does work in mysterious ways and has many means at His disposal to use to communicate with us!

The prayer uttered by Vera Resu at a graduation ceremony many years ago gives us another example of how God may give us a hint of the future in a wonderful way.

> In 1940, at a graduation ceremony held at the Florida Bible Institute, Vera Resu, class valedictorian, said, "At each critical epoch of the church, God has a chosen human instrument to

shine forth His light in darkness. Men like Luther, John and Charles Wesley, Moody, and others were ordinary men but men who heard the voice of God. It has been said that Luther revolutionized the world. It was not he, but Christ working through him. The time is ripe for another Luther, Wesley, and Moody. There is room for another in this list . . ."

Standing among the people in that graduating class was a young man who would go on to impact his world with the gospel. That young man was Billy Graham.[4]

When we give our lives to God and follow Him, He divinely leads us toward the future He has ordained for us. "'For I know the plans I have for you,' says the LORD. 'They are plans for good and not for disaster, to give you a future and a hope'" (Jer. 29:11 NLT).

See His Providence in Your Life

There are many ways in which God may choose to lead you. In some situations He clearly opens and shuts doors that channel us down certain paths. Revelation 3:7 says: "This is the message from the one who is holy and true. He is the one who has the key of David. He opens doors, and no one can shut them; he shuts doors, and no one can open them" (NLT).

An open door of providence is a green light—a welcome opportunity clearly indicating you should proceed forward. When the apostle Paul wrote to the Corinthian people, he told them about an open door that had been granted him by the Lord. He said, "But I will tarry in Ephesus until Pentecost. For a great and effective door has opened to me, and there are many adversaries" (1 Cor. 16:8–9).

Not all open doors are indications of God's will for your life. You must investigate each opportunity and test it biblically to ensure that God is in fact the one who is opening the door for you at this time. Once you are certain of God's working, then you can proceed, receiving God's blessings. Paul the apostle had a direct encounter with Christ, who assured him that He had opened the door in Ephesus for Paul to remain and preach.

A closed door is a red light or stop sign that keeps you from going forward to fulfill a planned goal or direction despite your most dogged attempts. This providential halt may come through a lack of resources, a solid no response to your suggestion, the termination of an opportunity, a long delay that makes the decision unfeasible, or the ending of a relationship. Again we must be sensitive to God's leading, because not all difficulties and trials are closed doors, though they may seem like it when we experience them.

Luke writes of a door that was closed to the apostle Paul and his party when they attempted to venture into Asia: "Now when they had gone through Phrygia and the region of Galatia, they were forbidden by the Holy Spirit to preach the word in Asia" (Acts 16:6). Although we do not know how the apostle Paul's little band of men were forbidden, we do know that through prayer God directed them another way, and the result was the proclamation of the gospel to what is now called the West or Western civilization.

Pay close attention to open and closed doors. God will often utilize this method to direct you toward His will. Psalm 25:4 says, "Show me the path where I should walk, O Lord; point out the right road for me to follow" (NLT).

In conjunction with open and closed doors, God "connects" us with people, places, and things for His glory, and He may use this form of leading with you.

God uses providential connections to effectively accomplish His goals, as we see in the Old Testament story of Ruth. Coming from a country called Moab, Ruth followed her mother-in-law, Naomi, back to Israel after the death of Naomi's husband and two sons. When they arrived, Ruth suggested that she begin to glean wheat in the field to provide food for their table. Let's see how God's providence unfolds in the following Scripture.

> Ruth the Moabitess said to Naomi, "Please let me go to the field, and glean heads of grain after him in whose sight I may find favor." And she [Naomi] said to her, "Go, my daughter." Then she left, and went and gleaned in the field after the reapers. And she *happened* to come to the part of the field belonging to Boaz, who was of the family of Elimelech. Now behold, Boaz came from Bethlehem, and said to the reapers, "The Lord be with you!" And they answered him, "The Lord bless you!" Then Boaz said to his servant who was in charge of the reapers, "Whose young woman is this?"
>
> Ruth 2:2–5, emphasis added

Notice how Ruth just happened to come to the field owned by Boaz. That was no accident! The path Ruth chose was controlled and directed by the divine hand of God. Boaz, who was related to Naomi, had the ability to marry Ruth, according to Judaic law. The story tells us that he exercised that option and eventually married Ruth. But that's not all. The couple had a child named Obed, who had a son named Jesse. Jesse was the father of David, who was the king of Israel, and it was through the line of David that Jesus Christ, the Messiah, came into the world.

When Ruth met Boaz in the field, it was the divine work of God's providence, engineered by the hand of God, not only to provide for Ruth and Naomi's needs but also to provide a marriage partner for Ruth and make way for the coming of the Messiah.

Have you ever experienced the providence of God in your life? God brings people across your path for a reason—often to help you walk in the direction He wants you to go. Daniel 4:3 says: "How great are His signs, and how mighty His wonders! His kingdom is an everlasting kingdom, and His dominion is from generation to generation."

God's Miraculous Providence

Every providential work of God is a miracle. Unfortunately, we do not often recognize them as such. For instance, if God closes or opens a door, if He puts together a monumental meeting or arranges a special promotion—we often fail to recognize that He has performed a miracle; we fail to thank Him for the wonderful work that He has done. We usually reserve the term *miracle* for that once-in-a-lifetime event. However, God is working miracles in our lives every day.

The following story about the classic hymn writer William Cowper illustrates God's miracle in his life though a seemingly common occurrence.

A story is told of the poet Cowper, who was subject to fits of great depression. One day he ordered a cab and had himself driven to the London Bridge. Soon, a dense fog settled down upon the city. The cabby drove about for two hours and then finally admitted that he was lost and could not find the London Bridge, even though he had been in the business for years. Cowper asked him if he could find the way home. He said that he could, and in an hour, landed Cowper at his door. When asked what the fare would be, the driver mentioned a sum, but said that he felt he ought not take anything since he had not filled his order. "Never mind," said Cowper. "You have saved my life. I was on my way to throw myself off the London Bridge." Cowper gave him double the usual fare. He then went into the house and wrote the hymn which bears the lines: "God moves in mysterious ways His wonders to perform, He plants His footsteps on the sea, and rides upon the storm."

God prevented Cowper from taking his own life through a series of "miracles," including a dense London fog and a confused cab driver. The result was a life lived for God and a hymn that, to this day, encourages people around the world.[5]

Daniel 6:27 says: "He rescues and saves his people; he performs miraculous signs and wonders in the heavens and on earth" (NLT). God cares for you and He is in control of your life. His providential works are for your good. However, you must recognize the signs and realize when they are authentically from Him.

God indeed works in miraculous ways, but we must always be careful not to try to turn God into a "genie in a bottle," a God who exists only to perform miracles in our lives and to relieve us of our critical responsibilities. On the other hand, there are many people who simply refuse to believe in the miraculous and in God's providence. They do not believe God works in supernatural ways, so they rely on themselves and human reasoning for everything.

Seek to have a sound, balanced, biblical view of the providential works of God in your life. Acknowledge the validity of miracles, but test all supernatural phenomena for biblical authenticity. The Bible has given you specific tests you can use to discern truth and deception.

Providence versus Wishful Thinking

Wishful thinking has led some people to interpret events in their lives as miraculous when, in fact, they are not miracles at all. Some proclaim that God has spoken to them about a business deal, a relationship, or a future event. We need to guard against self-deception and test each event or "prophecy" with God's Word. Much grief has been caused because of people who have claimed that God was behind their plans, programs, desires, and even ministries—when in reality He was not.

I once heard a story about a pastor who was preaching to his congregation about Bible study one Sunday morning and said: "If you use a word ten times, you will own it for life." As he continued preaching, a young woman was heard speaking softly in the last row: "Fred, Fred, Fred . . ."

Truly God does perform miracles today and works in our lives actively to accomplish His will, but we need to be careful that we do not replace His will with our wishes, which may be very different! How do we discern God's will from our own when they are in conflict? The Greek philosopher Socrates is known for the famous quote, "Know thyself." I believe that this is both wise and biblical! Therefore, first ask God for discernment concerning your heart and mind. You may want to consult Jeremiah 17:9–10 in this connection. Then take some time alone to examine your plans in the light of God's Spirit through prayer. Follow this with a request for counsel from some of your trusted friends. These are some of the ways in which we discern the difference between our own plans and those of God when they are in conflict.

Providence versus Probability

Probability by definition is the relative frequency with which an event occurs. When God causes an event to happen, it outweighs all probability! It may occur as a divine meeting, an open or closed door, or a miracle that cannot be otherwise explained. We should make sure when we call something miraculous that it is, in fact, an event that is not common or a mere coincidence. In other words, make sure there is little probability that the event would have occurred outside of God's divine intervention. "Test all things; hold fast what is good. Abstain from every form of evil" (1 Thess. 5:21–22).

Providence versus Powers of Darkness

So many people today are on a quest for divine guidance. Yet many are looking in all the wrong places, falling prey to wolves in sheep's clothing, including palm readers, mediums, astrologers, and even some who claim to worship Christ. Second Peter 2:3 says: "In their greed they will make up clever lies to get hold of your money. But God condemned them long ago, and their destruction is on the way" (NLT).

Events that appear miraculous can occur through the occult and at the hands of well-taught hucksters who operate under the false title of "spiritual leader." Be sure to test all signs and wonders and determine whether the powers of God or darkness are behind the circumstances you are facing. The Bible says Satan masquerades as an angel of light. In the end times there will be "lying wonders" energized by Satan to deceive those who reject the truth of God. The problem with such so-called miracles is that, on careful examination, they break down to nothing more than misleading tricks.

A miracle is a special act of God that interrupts the natural course of events in our world. Miracles have five basic components:

1. They are out-of-the-ordinary wonders that do not fit into the pattern of events in our natural world.
2. They are acts of God.
3. They have the distinctive purpose of glorifying God and providing evidence that He exists.
4. They have a moral dimension and result in goodness.
5. They bear fruit for God's kingdom.[6]

Be sure to use God's Word as the litmus test to determine right and wrong in all the spiritual matters of life. Don't be duped; stay with the original—Christ!

Providence and Destiny

"And we know that God causes everything to work together for the good of those who love God and are called according to his purpose for them" (Rom. 8:28 NLT).

Over the centuries men and women, guided by the light of God's Word, have seen their lives used for His glory. God's providence molded their destiny and changed the course of the world.

A story told by Christian evangelist and apologist Ravi Zacharias illustrates this well.

Hien Pham was a Vietnam translator to the U.S. armed forces during the Vietnam war. He was also a Christian and a missionary. After Vietnam fell to the Communists, Hien was arrested for aiding and abetting the Americans and was confined to prison. He was given Communist propaganda to read constantly and was prohibited from reading the Bible. The Communists' goal was to indoctrinate him against the West by cleansing his mind of democratic ideals and Christianity.

After a long time of only reading Communist writings and being exposed to horrible prison life, one day Hien decided to give up on Christ. "After all, maybe I have been lied to, and God does not exist, and the West has deceived me." Finally, he made up his mind and determined that, when he awakened the next day, he would not pray anymore and not think of his Christian faith again.

The next morning he was assigned to clean the latrines of the prison, which was the most dreaded chore, shunned by everyone. As he cleaned out a tin can overflowing with toilet paper, his eyes caught what he thought was English, printed on a piece of paper. He hurriedly washed it off and slipped it in his hip pocket, hoping to read it at night, not having seen anything in English in a long time.

When he pulled it out that evening with a flashlight in his cell, he was surprised when at the top corner he saw "Romans Chapter 8."

Literally trembling with shock, he began to read. "And we know that in all things God works for the good of those who love him, who have been called according to his purpose. Who shall separate us from the love of Christ? Shall trouble or hardship or persecution or famine or nakedness or danger or sword?" (Rom. 8:28). Hien wept, for he had not seen his Bible in so long—and he knew God had answered his prayer. He cried out to God, asking for forgiveness.

The next day and for some days to come, Hien volunteered to clean the latrines. Each day he found a new portion of Scripture. In this way, he retrieved a large portion of the Scriptures. He had determined that a commander in the camp was using the Bible as toilet paper!

The day came when, through a miracle, Hien was released from prison. And he was determined to escape from Vietnam. After several unsuccessful attempts, he planned to build a large boat in secret. With about fifty-three others, Hien was taking the lead until four days before the planned escape. The Vietcong knocked at his door.

When he opened the door, they accosted him and said that they had heard he was trying to escape. "Is it true?" they demanded. Hien denied it and went on to make up a story that he had concocted. Apparently convinced, the Vietcong reluctantly left.

Hien was relieved but very disappointed in himself. "Here I go again, Lord, trying to chart my own destiny, too unteachable in my own spirit to believe that You can lead me beyond any obstacle." He made a promise to God, fervently hoping that the Lord would not take him up on it. He prayed, if the Vietcong returned, he would tell them the truth, but rested assured they would never come back. But Hien was thoroughly shaken when only a few hours before setting sail, the four Vietcong stood at his door once more. "We have our sources. We know now that you are trying to escape. Is it true?" they asked.

Hien resignedly gave his answer: "Yes, I am, with fifty-three others. Are you going to arrest me and put me in prison?"

There was a pronounced pause and then they leaned forward and answered: "No, we want to escape with you!"

In an utterly incredible escape plan, all fifty-seven people got away but soon found themselves engulfed in high seas and a horrible storm. Hien buried his face in his hands and prayed, "God, did you bring us here to die?"

Later, he related this conclusion: If it were not for the sailing expertise of the Vietcong, the escapees never would have arrived safely to their destination—and eventually to America, where he resides today![7]

Digging Deeper: God's Intervention in Your Life

What miracles of providence has God brought forth for you? Has He brought people into your path who have helped guide you into His will? Has He opened and closed doors?

In your journal make note of the ways the Lord has worked supernaturally with you. Write down the ways God's providential acts have been helpful in leading you toward specific decisions you have had to make.

If you find yourself in a difficult place or in the center of a crisis, there is nothing wrong with praying for a miracle. Indeed, there are times in all of our lives when we truly need a miracle. Clearly it is not wrong to pray for one, as long as you are not trying to escape your own responsibility. Here's a good rule of thumb: Don't look for the miraculous, but welcome it when it comes!

Deuteronomy 3:24 says: "O Lord GOD, You have begun to show Your servant Your greatness and Your mighty hand, for what god is there in heaven or on earth who can do anything like Your works and Your mighty deeds?"

"The LORD says, 'I will make you wise and show you where to go. I will guide you and watch over you'" (Ps. 32:8 NCV).

7

Surrender

Living for God

A man speeding down the freeway was caught on film by an automated speed trap. Clocking his actual speed, the automated traffic cop also took a photograph of his car, including the license plate number. A few weeks later in his mailbox, the man received a speeding citation from the police department ordering him to pay forty dollars or show up in court.

The man was furious. So, to spite the police department, he cleverly photocopied two twenty-dollar bills and mailed the photocopies with his speeding ticket into the traffic court. One week later he received an envelope back from the traffic court. In it was a photocopy of a pair of handcuffs!

The man promptly sent in the real money for the ticket.

Many people try to pass off a photocopy instead of full surrender to God. Of all the keys to knowing the will of God, surrender probably ranks as the most important. In the valley of surrender we truly give God the right to direct our plans, bodies, minds, and hearts. It is in the valley of surrender that we meet God and find His divine will for our lives.

Yet surrender is also one of the hardest things for us to do because of our sin nature. With God's power, however, we can live for Him and walk in His will. Those who have lived exciting, vibrant, fulfilling lives have understood the principle of surrendering all to God. These people also have one thing in common. They have received God's best!

"I know, LORD, that a person's life is not his own. No one is able to plan his own course" (Jer. 10:23 NLT).

Surrender is your gateway to the will of God.

I beseech you therefore, brethren, by the mercies of God, that you present your bodies a living sacrifice, holy, acceptable to God, which is your reasonable service.

Romans 12:1

WHEN YOU SURRENDER your body, mind, will, and plans to God, you will discover the glorious will that He has for your life. However, when you venture out to live for God, one thing is clear: you will have a battle on your hands.

The process of surrendering to God, in any area of life, conflicts with the flesh (our human nature) and the world. Satan knows a surrendered life will glorify God and there's nothing he hates more. But take heart, for you are not alone in your struggles. With the help of the Holy Spirit, you have the power to surrender your life to Christ and to walk according to His will.

There's a War Raging

Military schools teach that the most important part of a battle occurs on the fronts. Indeed, no other part of war is as strategic as the battlefront. When ground is won on the battlefront, a strategic victory is given to the side that gained the ground. By gaining that foothold, the side that won the front often goes on to win the war.

There are three main battlefronts for Christians, each described in Romans 12:1–2: "I beseech you therefore, brethren, by the mercies of God, that you present your bodies a living sacrifice, holy, acceptable to God, which is your reasonable service. And do not be conformed to this world, but be transformed by the renewing of your mind, that you may prove what is that good and acceptable and perfect will of God."

Here are the three battlefronts:

1. the *body* (flesh), which can be open to sin because of its sinful bent and passionate desires
2. the *mind*, which is assaulted by the world system that rages against God
3. the *will*, which the enemy of our soul—Satan—comes against with the goal of destroying our lives by compelling us to reject God and His plans

The key to victory on each of these fronts is found in the power of our surrender to God. Let's take some time to address each battlefront and discuss the power God has given us to have victory over our enemies and to do His will.

Surrender Your Body

In today's world a war is being waged for the bodies of men and women. Virtually no corner of the earth has been left untouched by the ramifications and devastation of this battle. Sexual freedoms combined with the glamorization of the deeply sensual have resulted in a society gone wild.

In addition to the dangers of our sexually promiscuous society, violence and murder are commonplace. Crimes that were unthinkable twenty years ago are daily headlines. We are living in a world motivated by fear. At every level of society, anger has a foothold and can be seen regularly on our freeways. The old saying "It's a jungle out there" has become a scary reality.

Many people today resort to getting high on drugs and alcohol to escape the pressures of our world. Breweries that manufacture alcoholic beverages have become some of the largest corporations in the world, with sales reaching into the billions. Their advertising and sponsorship at sporting events around the globe are inescapable. Drinking and drug usage have become rampant in our culture.

The movie industry glamorizes self-destructive lifestyles. Today with the press of a button we can invite pornography and graphic violence right into our own homes and offices—at any time, twenty-four hours a day, seven days a week. Many children, who are so often the victims of this runaway world of ours, have direct access to these images on the Internet, being exposed to things that should never be viewed even by adults.

What will be the result of the downward moral spiral of global society? We are catapulting toward self-destruction and a virtual Sodom and Gomorrah scenario that is crying out for God's intervention.

Today many people are addicted to sinful lifestyles, having built patterns in their lives that they seem unable to overcome. But God wants to rid us of these destructive lifestyles. He wants us to live for Him by surrendering our bodies to Him.

The word *present*, as used in Romans 12:1, carries with it the connotation of a priest placing an offering on an altar, as in Old Testament times. Literally, it means "to surrender, yield up, stand beside, and be ready."

The idea of being ready is important, because temptation often appears out of nowhere, in an instant of time. Therefore, we must never lower our guard. We must be sober-minded and alert, ready to yield to God at all times. The picture of the Old Testament priest placing a sacrifice on the altar of God is beautiful as we consider making our own lives a presentation to the One who created us.

The word *present* is also a military term meaning "to stand beside, bring before, be ready, command, and yield." In essence, we are to raise a white flag before God in this battle for our bodies as we fight against the temptation to sin. As believers, we need to surrender our bodies at the cross of Christ.

A story called "History of the Iron Cross," beautifully illustrates the concept of presenting our bodies to God.

With the national coffers depleted from costly wars, King Frederic William III of Prussia found his nation seriously short of funds as it attempted to rebuild. He refused to give in to his enemies, and he couldn't face disappointing his people. So after considerable thought, he asked the women of Prussia to bring their gold and silver to be melted down and used in exchange for the things the nation desperately needed.

As each woman brought her jewelry, she was given a cross of bronze or iron as a symbol of the king's gratitude. On the cross were inscribed these words: "I gave gold for iron, 1813." The response was overwhelming. The women cherished their gifts from the king—even more than their former jewels!

The decorations were proof that they had sacrificed for their king. In fact, it became highly unfashionable in early nineteenth-century Prussia for women to wear any jewelry at all, except one piece of jewelry, which was the cross of iron.

And it was from this that the order of the Iron Cross was established.[1]

Just as the women had a motive to serve the Prussian king and to help build his kingdom, we too have a motive to offer our bodies in service to the King of all creation and His kingdom purposes. Our motive comes from our love for Christ for His sacrifice on Calvary's cross for our sins and our desire to be with Him eternally when this life ends, according to His promises in Scripture. The Prussian king had the power to melt down the silver and gold ornaments. Likewise, God has the power to melt our sinful desires and transform them into desires for Him. The king rewarded each donor with an engraved cross of her own, and we who have surrendered our lives to God will be rewarded, because we have our names engraved in the Lamb's Book of Life.

No matter what battle you are facing today, I urge you to come to the holy ground of Christ's cross, from where the very fountain of forgiveness flows and atones for your every sin. When you, in faith, surrender your body to God, you can be certain His power will go with you!

Surrender Your Mind

The influence of the world on our minds is overwhelming. Constantly, music, films, entertainment, and the arts bombard us with moral decadence. Fashion trends that catch the attention of our young people cater to immoral tastes. Pure language is also on a steady decline and is being replaced by illicit language, which can be heard daily on radio and TV and in the movies. Respect for others has become a thing of the past.

Today's ruling philosophy is self-indulgence. "You only go around once in life, so grab all the gusto you can." "Life is short. Go for it!" "It's a dog-eat-dog world out there; eat or be eaten." "He who dies with the most toys wins." "It's all about *me*." These are the popular slogans in our "self" belief system. The tragic result of all of this inward focus is that our love has grown cold. We have become a generation of angry, disrespectful, unforgiving, worrisome, cynical people. And this is not surprising. God's Word teaches us that when our minds are given over to self-centered living, the results can be the eventual destruction of the individual, the family, our children, and even the nation (see Isa. 5:1–30; Rom. 1:1–32).

Social scientists are calling our era "the age of anxiety." Neurosis is rampant. Worry has gripped the minds of millions. In fact today's most common prescription drugs target depression and anxiety disorders. How sad it is that the peace of God is available to all but attained by so few!

Many people have difficulty overcoming hatred, jealousy, anger, and worry, all of which have their root in the mind. Others admit to an inability to forgive because of the extreme bitterness that saturates their thoughts.

Perhaps you are struggling with one or several of these sins of the mind and heart. One thing is clear: Harboring sinful thoughts will have devastating effects on your life, leading to self-destruction. Worry, envy, jealousy, anger, bitterness, and an unforgiving spirit all work against you and can keep you from giving yourself to God and from receiving His divine will for your life.

Second Corinthians 10:5 says: "We capture every thought and make it give up and obey Christ" (NCV). The key to overcoming the sins of the mind is to have a mind controlled by Christ. We are to take captive those thoughts that war against our souls and attempt to distort the Word of God, weaken our faith, and bring our bodies into bondage.

Did you realize you could make these thoughts prisoners of war? Here's how: "Don't copy the behavior and customs of this world, but let God transform you into a new person by changing the way you think" (Rom. 12:2 NLT). The J. B. Phillips translation of this verse presents a descriptive image of what can happen to our minds: "Don't let the world around you squeeze you into its own mold, but let God remold your minds from within so that you may prove in practice that the plan of God for you is good, meets all his demands and moves toward the goal of true maturity" (Rom. 12:2 Phillips).

The Greek word for *transform* in this verse is the word from which we get our English word *metamorphosis*; it means "to change or transfigure." The transformation of a caterpillar into a beautiful butterfly is an excellent illustration of what happens to our minds by the power of God. Miraculously God transforms our minds so that we can have a spiritual understanding of His Word and have power to bring our thoughts under His divine influence.

There is a great movement in our world to steer far away from God and His principles. Those involved in this trend work diligently to attack all that is decent and right—and they battle for the minds of all people, especially children. The victor in this war is the one whose mind will not be taken captive by styles, trends, immorality, godless philosophy, hatred, and worry—all of which result in destruction.

Jesus Christ is the victor in the battle for the mind. Consider Jesus's reaction to those who mocked Him, spit on Him, and hung Him on the cross. He said, "Father, forgive them, for they do not know what they do" (Luke 23:34). How could He pray such a thing? There are several reasons: First, Jesus knew clearly the end from the beginning and that God had purposed good, even in His pain, agony, and death. Second, Jesus had hope in the Father's divine will for His life. Third, Jesus knew that His death would bear fruit, as thousands throughout the generations would be reconciled to God because of His work on the cross. Above all, Jesus could forgive because it was right and just according to God. Therefore, He who is holy set a standard for us.

Perhaps you are having a hard time forgiving your father or mother for what they did to you as a child. You could be suffering in an unhappy marriage in which you feel used and abused. Maybe you are the victim of a bad business venture, a crime committed against you, or a sister or brother who has wounded you. I urge you to take your thoughts captive, surrendering them daily to Christ and His cross. Go to God and ask Him to give you the power to forgive. That same power that was so wonderfully displayed by Christ on the cross is available for you today. "For the weapons of our warfare are not carnal but mighty in God for pulling down strongholds . . . bringing every thought into captivity to the obedience of Christ" (2 Cor. 10:4–5).

Let God, through His Word, renew and renovate your mind. This occurs spiritually as you know His Word and invite His Spirit to cleanse you from all of your impurities. Receive from Him a new set of glasses to see as the Creator sees. By faith, battle victoriously against those impure thoughts and bring every thought into the obedience of Christ. God has given you the power to choose pure thoughts, but you must take the initiative to ask Him to help you do it, while walking hand in hand with Him in His strength.

Surrender Your Will

Mark 12:30 tells us: "You must love the Lord your God with all your heart, all your soul, all your mind, and all your strength" (NLT). The Greek word for *heart* in the New Testament is a word that was used to describe the seat of the emotions and the will. Surrendering one's heart to God requires an act of the will, an act that is not easy, because it demands that we surrender all.

Practically speaking, when we talk about surrendering the will, we often speak in terms of personal plans, goals, and desires. Is your greatest desire in life to glorify God? Do you yearn with every ounce of your soul to follow His will? Have you placed your plans, efforts, ambitions, career, and relationships on the altar of Christ's sacrifice and said to

God, "Please, have Your way"? When you live your life in this manner, you are surrendering your will to God, and you will live out His will for your life and be blessed.

The life plans and goals we cherish are difficult to surrender to almighty God, because we deeply fear He may change our plans or, worse, shelve them altogether. However, when we fight for our own way and our own personal plans, without divine guidance, the result is usually a life of strife and unhappiness. When we choose to strive with our Maker, we will experience a thorny path.

But when we come to Christ and say, "I surrender all, take my life, use me for Your glory, and do with me as You please," then we begin to realize the blessing of the divine will of God and His direction.

Take Abram for an example. God appeared to him after he had been victorious in battle over several kings and rescued his wayward nephew, Lot, from harm. Genesis details the story for us.

> The LORD spoke to Abram in a vision and said to him, "Do not be afraid, Abram, for I will protect you, and your reward will be great."
> But Abram replied, "O Sovereign LORD, what good are all your blessings when I don't even have a son? Since I don't have a son, Eliezer of Damascus, a servant in my household, will inherit all my wealth. You have given me no children, so one of my servants will have to be my heir."
> Then the LORD said to him, "No, your servant will not be your heir, for you will have a son of your own to inherit everything I am giving you." Then the LORD brought Abram outside beneath the night sky and told him, "Look up into the heavens and count the stars if you can. Your descendants will be like that—too many to count!" And Abram believed the LORD, and the LORD declared him righteous because of his faith.
>
> Genesis 15:1–6 NLT

God promised Abram that an extraordinary miracle would occur and that he would become the father of a son. Abram and his wife, Sarai, waited for God to perform this miracle, but after many years, when nothing happened, they decided to do what seemed best to them. They decided to make God's promise happen by their own initiative: "'The LORD has kept me from having any children,' Sarai said to Abram. 'Go and sleep with my servant. Perhaps I can have children through her.' And Abram agreed" (16:2 NLT).

How creative they were! The results, however, were disastrous: "So Abram slept with Hagar, and she became pregnant. When Hagar knew she was pregnant, she began to treat her mistress Sarai with contempt. Then Sarai said to Abram, 'It's all your fault! Now this servant of mine is pregnant, and she despises me, though I myself gave her the privilege of sleeping with you. The LORD will make you pay for doing this to me!'" (vv. 4–5 NLT). The result of Abram and Sarai's refusal to surrender their plans to God and wait on His timing spelled major trouble on the home front.

"Abram replied, 'Since she is your servant, you may deal with her as you see fit.' So Sarai treated her harshly, and Hagar ran away. . . . So Hagar gave Abram a son, and Abram named him Ishmael. Abram was eighty-six years old at that time" (vv. 6, 15–16 NLT).

How telling these verses are concerning our own plans! Often hardship results when we are unwilling to surrender our plans to God. More than thirteen years passed before Abram heard from God again about the promised baby, and certainly during that intervening period Abram's home was filled with tension. However, God in His faithfulness visited Abram once again and told him that the child of the promise was going to be given to him and Sarai. "When Abram was ninety-nine years old, the LORD appeared to him and said, 'I am God Almighty; serve me faithfully and live a blameless life'" (17:1 NLT).

The thirteen-year delay in bringing the promise to Abram may have been a direct result of his and Sarai's refusal to surrender to God's original plan. How often do we spend days, months, and even years of our lives in vain, attempting to achieve our plans? If this has happened to you, don't panic, because God's gracious work is never through. You will find that He forgives, heals, and restores. He is the God of second chances!

"Then God added, 'Regarding Sarai, your wife—her name will no longer be Sarai; from now on you will call her Sarah. And I will bless her and give you a son from her! Yes, I will bless her richly, and she will become the mother of many nations. Kings will be among her descendants!' Then Abraham bowed down to the ground, but he laughed to himself in disbelief. 'How could I become a father at the age of one hundred?' he wondered. 'Besides, Sarah is ninety; how could she have a baby?'" (v. 15 NLT).

Proverbs 19:21 says: "You can make many plans, but the LORD's purpose will prevail" (NLT).

At this point, Abraham did something we are all prone to do when God's plans pierce a hole in our own. He asked God to change his mind. He pleaded with God to accept Ishmael as the promised son: "And Abraham said unto God, 'O that Ishmael might live before thee!' But God replied, 'Sarah, your wife, will bear you a son. You will name him Isaac, and I will confirm my everlasting covenant with him and his descendants'" (vv. 18–19 KJV).

Paul the apostle commented on Abraham's effort to argue with God when he wrote: "The Scriptures say that Abraham had two sons, one from his slave-wife and one from his free-born wife. The son of the slave-wife was born in a human attempt to bring about the fulfillment of God's promise. But the son of the freeborn wife was born as God's own fulfillment of his promise" (Gal. 4:22–23 NLT). Notice, Paul uses the words *human attempt* to describe the birth of Ishmael.

Let's stop trying to force our will and plans on God and instead, let Him do as He wills. Our heavenly Father knows best. Stop and think of all the tragedy that has been caused when people have taken matters into their own hands. God's grace alone is the solution to the problem—the antidote to the disease of self-will.

Is there an Ishmael living in your life today? Are you crying out to God, "O that Ishmael might live before You," in an effort to get your own way? Are you afraid of what it might mean to commit your life and will fully to God?

"Father, if you are willing, please take this cup of suffering away from me. Yet I want your will, not mine" (Luke 22:42 NLT). Jesus Christ prayed these words in the Garden just prior to His arrest and crucifixion. This prayer is perhaps one of the greatest in all of Scripture. Here, the Son of God, the God-Man, submits His will to the Father as a model—for all humanity to see. The subsequent sacrifice of His life was to be the greatest sacrifice in all of history.

God had become man and dwelt among us. He was sinless, perfect, and without guilt. He had healed all manner of horrible diseases, restored bodies, multiplied loaves and fish, calmed storms and seas, and even brought the dead back to life. The ultimate sorrow was being rejected by His own creation. However, the result of Christ's sacrifice was salvation for all humanity—all who would accept Jesus Christ as their Savior.

Abraham received the grace of God. In time Sarah became pregnant with a son whom she and Abraham named Isaac, a Hebrew word that means "laughter." They gave him that name because Sarah laughed when God told Abraham they would have a baby at nearly one hundred years of age (Gen. 18:12). But God fulfilled His promise, and today the nation of Israel exists as a result.

Will you surrender your human plans, expectations, and dreams to the One who can do the miraculous and who desires to bless you in extraordinary ways? Don't be afraid of surrendering. Instead, rejoice! God's plans for you are like those of a parent toward a child—they are good.

Surrender is a daily activity that begins with prayer. During prayer, surrender your body, mind, and will to God. In other words, say to God, "I will follow You wherever You lead. For Your will is my delight, Lord!"

The Battle Is the Lord's

How do you surrender? Maybe you are frustrated right now because you have tried and tried to overcome your sins but keep failing. Perhaps you are wondering if there is any hope for you. Not only is there hope, but there is also victory for your life. God has given you His grace to surrender completely to Him and His power to win the battle.

But you need God's power. When you yield your life to the Lord, His Spirit enables you to overcome and be victorious in the battles of life. Jesus promised a special dimension of spiritual power to all who ask in prayer. "But when the Holy Spirit has come upon you, you will receive power and will tell people about me everywhere—in Jerusalem, throughout Judea, in Samaria, and to the ends of the earth" (Acts 1:8 NLT).

As you present your body to God for His purposes, pray and ask Him for His spiritual power to overcome the sinful temptations in your life. God will give you the power you need to live for Him. He will fight the battle for you. You simply need to ask Him. Jesus said, "How much more your heavenly Father will give the Holy Spirit to those who ask him!" (Luke 11:13 NCV).

How will you know that you have His power? Will you feel something? Perhaps, but many do not feel anything. Will you become superholy overnight? Change is sometimes immediate, but with others it is gradual. Simply believe that God has given you His power. Receive His promises by faith. Trust that God is with you and then turn from sin. Surrender your body, mind, and will to God daily as an act of consecration to Him. Do it out of love for Him. It is the power of God, coupled with a surrendered life, that makes for *spiritual dynamite.* Galatians 5:22–23 says: "When the Holy Spirit controls our lives, he will produce this kind of fruit in us: love, joy, peace, patience, kindness, goodness, faithfulness, gentleness, and self-control" (NLT).

The battle for the surrender of your will can be tremendous. You can win the battle, however, when you have God's power and you yield your will to Him. The Spirit-filled life is one of power because God can and will transform it. With God's power working within you, you are not on your own in the battle. He saved you by the death of His Son on the cross. God has done it all; you must simply believe.

Many people find it hard to believe that Christ has done it all and all they have to do is receive His forgiveness. What about you? In spite of knowing about Christ, you may think, *How could God really forgive me?* You may believe that it's impossible. But, you see, this is the wonder of God; this is the remarkable thing about His grace toward humankind. Remember, God's salvation is a gift to you. It is free to everyone who believes. Accept the gift. He loves you and has chosen you. There is no one else to fill your shoes—you are unique and have a divine purpose. As amazing as it may seem, God chooses to use sinners who have been saved by grace.

Many people find it hard to forgive themselves. Maybe you live under a black cloud of self-condemnation where you are found guilty in your own mind—and condemned. Often this results in a holding pattern in which, because you are never able to forgive yourself, you hold yourself back from experiencing God's blessings in your life, or you simply check out of life altogether, watching from the sidelines.

If self-condemnation plagues your life, perhaps it's because you have established your own set of internal laws, your own ten commandments, so to speak. By these internal laws, you stand or fall—and it turns out you fall more than you stand. Here again, you must trust in God's forgiveness and grace—and in *His* program of salvation. He is the one who governs the universe, and you must abide by His Word, not your own. "God saved you by his special favor when you believed. And you can't take credit for this; it is a gift from God" (Eph. 2:8 NLT).

Some people who face God's program for salvation deny it, simply declaring: "I am good enough and I think God will accept me into His heaven." Such people are deceived and guilty of setting up their own salvation program.

In the Grip of His Grace

The word *grace* in Scripture means "a gift" and refers to the free gift of eternal life that God gives to us. There is nothing you can do to earn it. God's work of salvation is absolutely free and comes through faith in Christ alone.

Misunderstanding this all-important doctrine can keep us from experiencing God's divine will in our lives. Many people have missed out on the great blessings of walking with God simply because they cannot understand or believe that He can be so loving.

When you repent of your sins, know this: *You are forgiven!* "If we confess our sins, he will forgive our sins, because we can trust God to do what is right. He will cleanse us from all the wrongs we have done" (1 John 1:9 NCV).

Many people do not understand the goodness of God. "Does God really have a great plan for me? I don't believe it," you might say. "Look at my life; it's hopeless." This simply is not the truth. God has a wonderful plan for your life. Simply believe and accept it. "The thief's purpose is to steal and kill and destroy. My purpose is to give life in all its fullness" (John 10:10 NLT).

When you come to the true understanding that God has good things in store for you, that He forgives you of your sins and wants to bless you and use you in extraordinary ways, then you will come to the Lord in boldness and faith. Knowing the Word of God is really the bridge to grace. When you know the doctrines of God, you will be moved by His love for you. Remember: "God saved you by his special favor when you believed. And you can't take credit for this; it is a gift from God" (Eph. 2:8 NLT). When we understand and apply the dual principles of power and grace in our lives, the battle is won, and God begins to work in an extraordinary way.

Today, won't you ask for the power of the Holy Spirit to fill you and work in you to overcome sin? Then identify those sins that you will attempt to conquer through the power of His Spirit. They may be sins of the body, mind, or will—but they are all conquerable by God's power. Next, believe by faith in the grace of God, and trust that God can use you—just as you are, right where you are.

Surrender

Romans 12:2 states the result of surrendering our bodies and minds to God so we may "prove what is that good and acceptable and perfect will of God." The Greek word for *prove* means "to discover, find out, or learn by experience." In this case we are discovering the will of God for our lives.

Another translation of Romans 12:1–2 may help to clarify this principle: "And so, dear Christian friends, I plead with you to give your bodies to God. Let them be a living and holy sacrifice—the kind he will accept. When you think of what he has done for you, is this too much to ask? Don't copy the behavior and customs of this world, but let God transform you into a new person by changing the way you think. Then you will know what God wants you to do, and you will know how good and pleasing and perfect his will really is" (NLT).

Did you note the end of the verse? *"Then you will know what God wants you to do!"* The result of surrender is the discovery of His will for your life—and how good it is. As you become open to His will, the Lord is able to bring things your way that are both new and exciting. Your heart becomes an open channel by which the streams of His desires can flow together with your own to bring you to the shores of His goodness and perfect will.

Will you yield to Him today? God has such grand plans for your life. I invite you to do some deep soul-searching. Ask God to perform spiritual surgery on your heart, mind, and will. Ask Him to bring you to the place where you are ready to let His will be done in you. You will find that surrendering to God is the gateway to His will, which brings happiness and joy to your life. Many have entered that gateway. I pray you will too.

Alexander Maclaren, the great Scottish pastor, said: "To know beyond doubt that I ought to do these things seems to me to be heaven on earth, and the man that has God's Word needs but little more."[2]

This sentiment is reflected in Psalm 40:5: "O LORD my God, you have done many miracles for us. Your plans for us are too numerous to list. If I tried to recite all your wonderful deeds, I would never come to the end of them" (NLT).

Do you still need some convincing? Consider the following stories:

- When the famous surgeon Howard Kelly graduated from medical school, he wrote in his diary, "Today I dedicate myself, my time, my capabilities, and my ambitions, everything to Christ. Blessed Lord, sanctify me to Thy uses. Give me no worldly success which may not lead me nearer to my Savior."

- Florence Nightingale wrote in her diary concerning surrender: "I am thirty years of age; the age in which Christ began His mission. Now, no more childish things, no more vain things." Years later, near the end of her heroic life of service, she was asked the secret of her ability to accomplish so much for the Lord. Her reply, "I can only give one explanation and that is this: I have kept nothing back from God."

- Soon after graduating from college, Jim Elliot wrote in his diary, "God, I pray to Thee, light these idle sticks of my life that I may burn for Thee. Consume my life, God, for it is Thine. I seek not a long life but a full one like You, Lord Jesus." God answered that prayer and in the zest of young manhood, Jim Elliot's life was cut short by the spear of an Auca Indian as he and several other young people sought to take the Gospel deep into the jungles of Ecuador. Through his death, the Auca Indians and many others have come to know Jesus Christ as their Savior.[3]

All of us have engaged in warfare against sinful desires and thoughts. We have all sinned and fallen short of God's standard and felt the weight of sin on our lives and consciences. God wants to pick us up, comfort us, forgive us, and show us the way to victory.

Today won't you yield your life to Him in faith, depend on His power to overcome, and trust in His grace?

Surrender is the pathway to realizing the God-given desires of your heart.

Digging Deeper: Choosing to Surrender

Thinking It Through

In your journal make note of the areas of surrender that are most critical for you. These will likely include sinful tendencies, but they also may include such needs as staying power in the midst of a difficult situation or relationship. Then begin to categorize these areas under the biblical headings of Romans 12:1–2:

Surrender my body. Read 1 Corinthians 6:19; Galatians 5:19–21; Colossians 3; and 1 Thessalonians 4.

Surrender my mind. Read 2 Corinthians 10; Galatians 5:19–21; and Philippians 1–4. In the book of Philippians, you may want to underline the word *mind* and study these verses. List those areas of the mind that you want to conquer.

Surrender my will. Read the book of Jonah—a great study in God's will. List those areas of your will that you are having trouble delivering up to God. Is there a goal or dream you are unwilling to turn over to God?

Practical Action

Are there any areas that are standing in the way of your ability to surrender to God? Cherished music, media, literature, and possessions can be hurdles to your surrender. Relationships can also interfere with complete surrender to God. Make sure you are following God's Word in your marriage and in friendships. Keep in mind that forgiveness is often the key to godly relationships.

Carefully evaluate each area of your private and public life, and then determine how to deal with them biblically. You may want to enlist the help of a Christian mentor or your pastor to receive wise counsel.

Remember, God wants to be the main object of your desire!

"Then Jesus said to the disciples, 'If any of you wants to be my follower, you must put aside your selfish ambition, shoulder your cross, and follow me. If you try to keep your life for yourself, you will lose it. But if you give up your life for me, you will find true life'" (Matt. 16:24–25 NLT).

8

Courage

Making the Decision

*A Texas billionaire hosted a sumptuous feast on his 1,500–
acre property outside of Dallas. He took the guests for a
complete tour of his land, horse stables, and mansion. As he
came to the end of the tour, the guests were ushered to the
back of the mansion to plush lawns sporting beautifully
landscaped scenes and a giant swimming pool, the likes of
which none of them had seen before. However, after closer
review, the guests noticed that the glistening pool was filled
with huge alligators.*

*"Why do you have a pool full of alligators?" one of the
shocked guests asked.*

*"It takes courage to make your mark in this world," answered
the billionaire. "So I keep this pool of alligators on my*

property as a sign of what courage really is. In fact I tell all my guests, anyone who has enough guts to jump in the pool and swim safely shall be entitled to half my fortune and to my only daughter as his wife."

The guests began to laugh until suddenly they heard a splash. All eyes became fixed on a young man swimming across the pool. Incredibly, he made it across to the other side and got out.

The guests were astounded; the billionaire was dumbfounded.

"I'm impressed," he said. "Son, you are entitled to half my fortune and my only daughter as your wife."

Wet from head to toe and bleeding from minor scratches, the young man replied, "Sir, you can keep your fortune and your daughter. What I want to know is: Who pushed me in?"[1]

When we come to that all-important moment we call "decision time," we often feel like the young man in the pool, and we want to cry out, "Who pushed me in?"

Whether it's signing on the dotted line to buy a new home or commit to a major contract, walking down the aisle for marriage, or moving across country—there is a lot riding on each major decision we make in life. Not only is our future on the line, but also our time, money, relationships, and most of all, the possibility that we may fail.

Life decisions can be tough! We need courage to decide.

I command you—be strong and courageous! Do not be afraid or discouraged. For the LORD your God is with you wherever you go.

Joshua 1:9 NLT

NOW WE COME to decision-crunch time. In this chapter we will explore six critical keys to making successful decisions while also exploring an old master's formula for knowing the will of God. I pray that this chapter will help you pull together all that's been said thus far into a well-packaged system that will enable you to make wise, God-directed decisions.

Key Principle 1—The Need for Peace

"And let the peace that comes from Christ rule in your hearts" (Col. 3:15 NLT). The word translated *rule* in this verse is Greek for "garrison, arbitrate, or govern." The term *garrison* is a military term referring to the guarding of a fortress with troops. The words *arbitrate* and *govern* describe the role of direction in the decision-making process. This verse tells us that when God intervenes in our lives with his complete protection, sure guidance, and deep wisdom, the result is our peace.

God's peace has been described in various ways: tranquility, inner peace, or even a gut feeling from God that confirms His will. However you choose to describe peace, the fact is—when you have it, you know it. And likewise, when you lack it, you know it.

Some weeks ago I was speaking to a prominent businessman whom I admire, a devout and humble believer in Jesus Christ and the retired CEO of a large multinational corporation. As we were having lunch, I asked this man how he had arrived at such a position in life. His answer was impressive: "Gary," he said, "throughout my life, God has given me little nudges and gut feelings to direct me. As I have lived my life before Him, I have often sensed at different times the direction God wants me to go, and those moves that He has directed me in have turned out for good. How else would I have arrived at becoming the CEO of such a large corporation if it weren't for God?"

During the decision-making process, you need to sit down and ask yourself one vital question: *Am I truly at peace with the direction I plan to take?* When you do not feel peace about a decision, stop and consider why. The lack of peace often serves as a warning signal telling you to stop, to wait.

You can ask God to guide you by His peace in any situation. Though peace is not the only way to know the will of God, once you have used God's Word in the decision-making process, peace often serves as the icing on the cake and can help you feel certain about a particular path.

My wife and I once attended a presentation for a time-share resort in Florida. The company put us up for three days at a nice resort, which included food and perks for almost nothing. All we were obligated to do was attend a one-hour sales presentation. If we did not want to buy the timeshare, we could pass and keep the free vacation. It was a good presentation and seemed like a great and inexpensive investment. As we were getting ready to sign, we told the salesman we would first like to think it over for the evening. We did not feel completely at peace about the decision, and the sales presentation did not entirely convince us. We prayed and that night went to the pool to relax. It was at the pool that we "providentially" met a nice couple.

By coincidence, they were there that weekend to try to sell the timeshare they owned. In fact, they owned three timeshares in three different resorts around the world and gladly offered us their counsel. They said, "We are trying to sell this one because we do not like the contractual arrangements. We would advise you to look elsewhere." After a long meeting with these seasoned vacation property owners, we were convinced not to buy at that location. It was a good thing we decided to wait and pray, even when the salesman had applied his famous "closing" pressure. We finished the vacation with joy.

Major decisions require a great deal of courage. There comes a time, after you've weighed all the options in God's Word, prayed, and sought His direction, when you need to resolve in your heart and mind that it's time to move forward. God's peace helps you confirm your heartfelt decision and gives you the confidence to say, "Yes, I am going to go for it. I'm ready!"

Key Principle 2—The Need for God's Perfect Timing

"Enthusiasm without knowledge is not good. If you act too quickly, you might make a mistake" (Prov. 19:2 NCV). Haste in decision making can often lead to negative results, but we may be hasty because of fear. When in a storm, the tendency is to rush to get out. As the old saying goes, "People will take any port in a storm!" People rush headlong into hasty decisions because they want to complete a goal, only to find that the right choice was just around the corner.

One of the wisest decisions we can make in life is to stop and wait. Few things in life are more rewarding than seeing a situation improve, watching prices drop, stocks rise, resolutions unfold, doors to better opportunities open, and doors to unwise options close—all because we decided to wait.

The history of Waterloo is inspiring in this regard.

June 18, 1815—one of world history's most decisive days. Napoleon had just left the island of Elba, where he had been rebuilding his army from exile. Sailing back to the mainland of Europe with him were 75,000 soldiers, including the Old Guard—perhaps the finest fighting men in the world. Although the Duke of Wellington, Commander-in-Chief of the British forces, offered to do his best to stop Napoleon, it seemed like a futile assignment.

At Waterloo, with only 67,000 allied troops, Wellington engaged Napoleon in battle. If Napoleon, who was heavily favored to win, were indeed victorious, there would have been no stopping him in his drive to conquer all of Europe. The people in England waited for hours as the battle raged. Eager for news, they had a ship waiting in the channel, which would signal the outcome of the contest to watchmen stationed in towers along the shores of Dover.

Finally, as planned, the signal ship did indeed manage to flag a message to the towers before becoming enshrouded in a fog bank: "Wellington defeated." The heart of the watchmen sank, but they relayed the word quickly to the waiting messengers and the words spread like wildfire throughout England: "Wellington defeated."

Hopelessness and despair set in as the British knew it would only be a matter of time before Napoleon would sail across the Channel and lay claim to their country.

However, after some time had passed and the fog lifted, the signal ship fired a cannon to get the attention of those in the tower. Flags flew again to reveal the third and final word of the message, "Napoleon." The entire message now read: "Wellington defeated Napoleon."

What a difference was made after the fog had lifted. The hearts of the British people rejoiced. "Napoleon has been stopped! We shall remain a free people!" Time—and a third word—filled their hearts with great joy.[2]

Sometimes, just a little time and a seemingly minor addition from God can generate the courage needed to move ahead and have victory.

You can save a great amount of time, effort, and discouragement by asking yourself a few questions before embarking on a new path in life: *Does this decision need to be made now? Am I the one to make this decision? Would it be best to wait? What are the pros and cons of waiting?* These vital questions often go unasked in the decision-making process, and unfortunately, failure may then result.

A good rule of thumb is to list the reasons why this is the best time to make your decision. Pray and ask God for His perfect timing in all matters. God knows the right time, and you can too. Consider, wait, and pray. Ecclesiastes 3:1 says: "There is a time for everything, a season for every activity under heaven" (NLT).

Key Principle 3—The Need for Rest

"He lets me rest in green meadows; he leads me beside peaceful streams" (Ps. 23:2 NLT). In our fast-paced society, it's quite possible to live life without ever making time for rest, relaxation, or contemplation.

Vince Lombardi, the legendary coach of the Green Bay Packers, once said, "Fatigue makes a coward of us all." What a great truth this is! Therefore, it is a good rule of thumb to never make a decision under the pressure of fatigue or burnout. If you are caught in a rut, always going but never stopping for a moment to consider where you are headed, you may be in danger. Without rest and time for contemplation you can lose your bearings and your sense of destiny. God desires to guide you to lie down in green meadows and rest beside still waters.

According to a Greek legend, in ancient Athens a man noticed the great storyteller Aesop playing childish games with some little boys. He laughed and jeered at Aesop, asking him why he wasted his time in such frivolous activity.

Aesop responded by picking up a bow, loosening its string, and placing it on the ground. Then he said to the critical Athenian, "Now answer the riddle, if you can. Tell us what the unstrung bow implies."

The man looked at it for several moments but had no idea what point Aesop was trying to make. Aesop explained, "If you keep a bow always bent, it will break eventually; but if you let it go slack, it will be more fit for use when you want it."

People are also like that. That's why we all need to take time to rest.[3]

Sometimes the answers to life's problems can become crystal clear as you walk along a windy beach or hike a mountain to get alone with God. He ordained the Sabbath day for rest for a reason. He knew you would need time to think and be alone with Him. One of the very best things you can do, therefore, before you say yes or no to a major decision is to take some time alone in total rest with God. Rest and relaxation, combined with a worshipful time with God, will help clear your mind and put life and its pressing matters into perspective. Physical exercise also helps you think more clearly as it releases tension from the body. God encourages rest: "You chart the path ahead of me and tell me where to stop and rest" (Ps. 139:3 NLT).

Key Principle 4—The Need for Resolve

Jesus's resolve to accomplish His mission is seen in Hebrews 10:7: "Then I said, 'Behold, I have come—in the volume of the book it is written of Me—to do Your will, O God.'"

Why is the topic of God's will so fascinating? The answer can be found in one word: *self*. We love to think about ourselves, talk about ourselves, and cater to ourselves. Be honest. Don't you—along with everyone else on the planet—long for happiness, gratification, contentment, and prosperity? Usually, choosing between self-will and God's will is a battle for most of us. Therefore, let us learn one solid principle. In the decision-making process, resolve first to accept God's will in your life despite what it may cost. In the end you shall have His best. When your motivation for life is within the will of God, then He can do for you what He has always wanted to do.

At the beginning of his reign, King Solomon resolved in his heart to put God first in his life. God honored his choice. Here is what happened in a divine encounter between King Solomon and God:

> At Gibeon the LORD appeared to Solomon in a dream by night; and God said, "Ask! What shall I give you?"
>
> And Solomon said: "You have shown great mercy to Your servant David my father, because he walked before You in truth, in righteousness, and in uprightness of heart with You; You have continued this great kindness for him, and You have given him a son to sit on his throne, as it is this day. Now, O LORD my God, You have made Your servant king instead of my father David, but I am a little child; I do not know how to go out or come in. And Your servant is in the midst of Your people whom You have chosen, a great people, too numerous to be numbered or counted. Therefore give to Your servant an understanding heart to judge Your people, that I may discern between good and evil. For who is able to judge this great people of Yours?"
>
> And the speech pleased the LORD, that Solomon had asked this thing. Then God said to him: "Because you have asked this thing, and have not asked long life for yourself, nor have asked riches for yourself, nor have asked the life of your enemies, but have asked for yourself understanding to discern justice, behold, I have done according to your words; see, I have given you a wise and understanding heart, so that there has not been anyone like you before you, nor shall any like you arise after you. And I have also given you what you have not asked: both riches and honor, so that there shall not be anyone like you among the kings all your days."

> 1 Kings 3:5–13

God wants your worship and your heart first—not your personal requests. After all, He knows your needs before you even ask Him: "For your Father knows the things you have need of before you ask Him" (Matt. 6:8).

Have you resolved in your heart to do God's will in your life despite what it may cost you personally? Christ's resolve speaks so clearly when, in making the final decision to give His life for the sins of the world, He prays: "My Father, if it is not possible for this painful thing to be taken from me, and if I must do it, I pray that what you want will be done" (Matt. 26:42 NCV).

Can you pray like this concerning the decision you are about to make? Ask yourself, *Am I neutral concerning this decision? Am I open to whatever might occur once the decision is made? Do I desire God's outcome and not my own?*

I encourage you to get on your knees at this moment and declare that you will unreservedly give your heart, mind, and will to God in every decision. If this is your motivation, you will experience the glorious will of God. And He will respond to your commitment by giving you the spiritual power and courage to do His will. "For it is God who works in you both to will and to do for His good pleasure" (Phil. 2:13).

Key Principle 5—The Need for Wisdom

"I have taught you in the way of wisdom; I have led you in right paths. When you walk, your steps will not be hindered, and when you run, you will not stumble" (Prov. 4:11–12). Walking according to the will of God and knowing the signs of His divine guidance require wisdom. I love the wisdom of God because it is so simple and yet so profound. Typically, when God is guiding me, I sense a desire in my heart. Some describe it as a deep burden, longing, or nudge from God to step out in faith and do something. When I sense this nudge, I go to prayer, asking God to guide me as

I begin to move forward in faith. Once in motion, I look for the providential guidance of God. Open and closed doors are important here.

Closed doors mean to me that this may not be the direction God has purposed, or perhaps it may not be His perfect timing. If I continue to experience closed doors as I am moving forward in faith, I will step back. Sometimes, in such a situation, God wants us to continue praying because it is not His timing. You may wonder why God would withhold from me the very desire He has given me. Often God wants us to grow in this waiting period. He may have spectacular things for our lives, but He must prepare us to handle them when they come. He may also be preparing other people to join us in the enterprise. He is crafting all the circumstances of life in the entire universe in preparation for the day when He will open doors for us. Therefore, I take heart when doors are closed for a time.

As I move through an open door, I always test to see what lies on the other side. Normally, when I am in the will of God, other people (like close friends, family, and sometimes even strangers) will be there to confirm that God is indeed working in my life. It is always comforting to know that God is at work in this way.

When I sense that a door is open, I really want to know who opened it. Was it God, other people, or me? You see, I am quite industrious, just like you, and can open my own doors when I really try. In their excitement friends have sometimes opened doors for me, but I found God had different plans. But when God opens a door, there is confirmation, and I know it deep in my heart.

When William Wilberforce came to faith through the "Great Change" that was his experience of conversion in 1785 at the age of twenty-five, his first reaction was to throw out politics and enter the ministry. He thought, as millions have thought before and since, that "spiritual" affairs are far more important than "secular" affairs.

Fortunately, a minister—John Newton, the converted slave trader who wrote "Amazing Grace"—persuaded Wilberforce that God wanted him to stay in politics rather than enter the ministry. "It's hoped and believed," Newton wrote, "that the Lord has raised you up for the good of the nation." After much prayer and thought, Wilberforce concluded that Newton was right. God was calling him to champion the liberty of the oppressed—as a Parliamentarian. "My walk," he wrote in his journal in 1788, "is a public one. My business is in the world; and I must mix in the assemblies of men, or quit the post which Providence seems to have assigned me."[4]

Listen for God's voice in your life; consider the desires or burdens He has placed on your heart; pray for God's confirmation; step out in faith; look for open and closed doors of providence; test those open doors to make sure they are from God; then seek wise counsel from others. These are just a few steps you must take as you travel the road called God's will. These same tried and true steps will be rehearsed in a more detailed way when we look later at the life of George Mueller. We need wisdom as we navigate our way on this journey to know the will of God. Pray and ask God for wisdom. "If you need wisdom—if you want to know what God wants you to do—ask him, and he will gladly tell you. He will not resent your asking" (James 1:5 NLT).

Key Principle 6—The Need for Courage

Most decisions in life will require courage. In fact most worthwhile ventures entail a great amount of risk. Those who are faint of heart are not comforted by this prospect. It may scare you to consider taking a leap into what appears to be darkness. But that may be what's required before any doors of opportunity swing open.

The biblical history of Joshua crossing the Jordan in the bold and dangerous conquest of Canaan provides a fitting illustration. It demonstrates how God permits challenges that lead to risk in our lives so we can learn to trust Him in deeper and greater ways.

In ancient times, the river Jordan was a formidable and dangerous barrier for any army to cross if they wanted to get into the land of Canaan. Joshua and his army of thousands would have to cross that river to conquer the land. But how could an army of thousands cross such a deep and wide river? God gave instructions to Joshua, the general of Israel's army, to command the priests of Israel to bear the ark of the covenant, containing the laws of God on tablets of stone, down to the Jordan River. Then the priests were to place their feet firmly in the water. When the priests' feet were in the water, God would move them to the next step.

God's miraculous response to Israel's faith is recounted in picturesque terms in the Old Testament book of Joshua.

> So it was, when the people set out from their camp to cross over the Jordan, with the priests bearing the ark of the covenant before the people, and as those who bore the ark came to the Jordan, and the feet of the priests who bore the ark dipped in the edge of the water (for the Jordan overflows all its banks during the whole time of harvest), that the waters which came down from upstream stood still, and rose in a heap very far away at Adam, the city that is beside Zaretan. So the waters that went down into the Sea of the Arabah, the Salt Sea, failed, and were cut off; and the people crossed over opposite Jericho. Then the priests who bore the ark of the covenant of the LORD stood firm on dry ground in the midst of the Jordan; and all Israel crossed over on dry ground, until all the people had crossed completely over the Jordan.
>
> Joshua 3:14–17

It is not unusual for God to work this way. Often He requires your first step to be into the unknown. Courage is needed to take those giant steps of faith. But when you know in your heart that you have followed the principles contained in Scripture and you have God at your side, there is nothing to fear. You will have the same results as the priests: They stood firm on dry ground. Once you have stepped out in faith, you will find that the flaming torch of God sheds light on the path you take, giving guidance for the next step.

Many decisions require that you take initiative. You must send out that résumé, perform that necessary research, go out and get that special counsel, meet that new person you have been afraid to meet, ask that lady out for a date, take one more trip out to see if that is the right place to live, make that offer, or send in that academic application. Take the first step.

Do not let risk or the possibility of failure scare you. As the old saying goes, "Better to have tried and failed than never to have tried at all." Get up and go. Even for the faint of heart, life requires that you take steps of faith, often with little or no insight from God whatsoever. Nearly everybody wants God to give direction before taking a leap of faith, but He is often silent until after you make the first move.

If you search for excuses—reasons for delay—you will always find them. Beware of justifying delay with false reasoning. Fear, laziness, and pride can masquerade as many worthy reasons to bail out. Search out the motivations of your heart.

Often we are surprised to find out that many of the world's greatest men and women had to overcome great disability and adversity to go on to greatness. Their lives teach us that circumstances do not make us what we are but reveal who we are.

Cripple him, and you have a Sir Walter Scott. Lock him in a prison cell, and you have a John Bunyan. Bury him in the snows of Valley Forge, and you have a George Washington. Raise him in abject poverty, and you have an Abraham Lincoln. Subject him to bitter religious prejudice, and you have a Benjamin Disraeli. Strike him down with infantile paralysis, and he becomes a Franklin D. Roosevelt. Burn him so severely in a schoolhouse fire that the doctors say he will never walk again, and you have Glenn Cunningham, who set the world's record in 1934 for running a mile in 4 minutes, 6.7 seconds. Deafen a genius composer, and you have Ludwig von Beethoven. Have him or her born black in a society filled with racial discrimination, and you have a Booker T. Washington, a Harriet Tubman, a Marian Anderson, or a George Washington Carver. Make him the first child to survive in a poor Italian family of eighteen children, and you have Enrico Caruso. Have him born of parents who survived a Nazi concentration camp, paralyze him from the waist down when he is four, and you have an incomparable concert violinist, Itzhak Perlman. Call him a slow learner, "retarded," and write him off as uneducable and you have an Albert Einstein.[5]

I urge you to move forward with your dreams, desires, and decisions with courageous power. There will always be reasons for not attempting a new course in life, but the saddest people of all are often those who have never tried. Once you have gone through the biblical steps of knowing God's will and have determined that you need to take a leap of faith, don't hold back! The old saying still holds true: "Nothing ventured, nothing gained."

Mueller's Method

George Mueller was the founder and director of a large orphanage in the 1800s in Bristol, England. He carried on his ministry by simple faith, to the amazement of the entire world. He was one of the spiritual giants of the preceding century, and at the peak of his ministry, the orphanage grew to two thousand children, and each child was provided food, clothing, and education all the way through high school.

During the course of his lifetime, Mueller trusted God completely to meet the needs of the orphanage (without fund-raising). Through gifts the orphanage received more than 7.5 million dollars for the provision of the children. On today's scale, that would equal nearly one hundred million dollars!

At the age of seventy-five, George Mueller left the orphanage to speak to audiences about God's provision and the need for faith. He traveled the world speaking until he died. His life exemplifies trust in God and satisfaction with His will. Today many who endeavor to live for God use Mueller's life as a model.

Prior to starting the orphanage, George Mueller sought the Lord's will for his life. He writes about the process for determining God's will: "First, I seek at the beginning to get my heart into such a state that it has no will of its own in regard to a given matter." (Nine-tenths of our trouble with discerning God's will is right here in Mueller's statement—our hearts need to be ready to do the Lord's will completely.) "When one is truly in this state, it is usually but a little way to the knowledge of what His will is. Second, having done this, I do not leave the result to feeling or to a single impression. If I do so, I make myself liable to great delusions." (Notice the wisdom in this statement. There is a need for patience and discernment when seeking out the will of God.)

Mueller continues to describe the process:

> Third, I seek the will of the Spirit of God through or in connection with the Word of God. The Spirit and the Word must be combined. If I look to the Spirit alone without the Word, I lay myself open to great delusions also. If the Holy Spirit guides us at all, He will do it according to the Scriptures and never contrary to them.

Fourth, I take into account providential circumstances. These often plainly indicate God's will in connection with His Word and Spirit.

Fifth, I ask God in prayer to reveal His will aright to me. Thus through prayer, the study of the Word and reflection, I come to a deliberate judgment according to the best of my ability and knowledge. And if my mind is thus at peace and continues so after two or three more petitions, I proceed accordingly. In trivial matters and in transactions involving most important issues, I have found this method always effective.[6]

George Mueller was a man who knew God's will. His method for coming to that knowledge can be boiled down to the following:

- First, surrender your will.
- Second, seek the Spirit's will through God's Word.
- Third, note providential circumstances.
- Fourth, pray for guidance.
- Fifth, wait on God.

Tests of Courage

If you have followed the steps for determining God's will but still don't see a clear path regarding God's direction in a particular situation, don't be discouraged. You will need courage to attempt great things in life. Often there will be obstacles that seem like mountains, but God will help you and lift you up along the way. He has something spectacular for you, even if you are presently suffering or if you are facing seemingly impossible odds.

The history of mountain explorer George Mallory, who led an expedition in an attempt to conquer Mount Everest in the 1920s, is an excellent example of courage.

The English adventurer had made his first expedition and failed. He then tried again, and the second time he failed as well. Mallory made a third assault with the highly skilled and experienced team. But in spite of careful planning and extensive safety measures, an avalanche wiped out Mallory and most of his party.

Upon their return to England, the few who had survived held a banquet to salute Mallory and those who had perished on the mountain. As the 23-year-old leader of the survivors stood to speak, he looked around the hall at the framed picture of Mallory and the others who had died, and he turned his back to the crowd and faced a large picture of Mount Everest which stood looming behind the banquet table like a silent unbeatable giant. With tears streaming down his face, he spoke to the mountain on behalf of his dead friends, "I speak to you Mount Everest in the name of all brave men living and those yet unborn. Mount Everest you defeated us once, you defeated us twice, you even defeated us three times; but Mount Everest, we shall some day defeat you, because you can't get any bigger but we can."[7]

Today when you look at the mountains that stand between you and your goals—the mountains of trials, the mountains of difficulty, the mountains of poor odds, the mountains of family history, the mountains of sinful temptation, the mountains of satanic opposition—I tell you that there is *no* mountain that can stand between you and God's will.

In the mid-1800s, there was a famed acrobat named Blondin, known for his death-defying stunts. One such stunt, for which he was famous, was to cross Niagara Falls on a tightrope. He did this four different times to the astonishment of a growing crowd.

The first time, he walked across the tightrope and the crowd began to grow. The second time, he walked across the tightrope while eating an omelet. The crowd grew larger. The third time, he walked across the tightrope carrying his manager. The crowd was now swelling.

The fourth time, he placed a wheelbarrow next to the tightrope, and the crowd began to cheer, "You can do it, Blondin. Go for it!" Blondin replied, "How many believe I can do it?" Everyone in the crowd raised their hands and continued to cheer and say, "We know you can do it!" He then asked, "Who will go in the wheelbarrow with me?"

Silence fell across the crowd as all hands dropped.

Remember, when you are crossing the tightrope of life, Jesus Christ will be with you!

> Can anything separate us from the love Christ has for us? Can troubles or problems or sufferings or hunger or nakedness or danger or violent death? As it is written in the Scriptures: "For you we are in danger of death all the time. People think we are worth no more than sheep to be killed." But in all these things we have full victory through God who showed his love for us. Yes, I am sure that neither death, nor life, nor angels, nor ruling spirits, nothing now, nothing in the future, no powers, nothing above us, nothing below us, nor anything else in the whole world will ever be able to separate us from the love of God that is in Christ Jesus our Lord.
>
> Romans 8:35–39 NCV

I pray today that you will take these words to heart. Memorize them and believe.

Chuck Swindoll, in his book *Seasons of Life*, wrote about courage.

> David had it when he grabbed his sling in the Valley of Elah. Daniel demonstrated it when he refused to worship Nebuchadnezzar's statue in Babylon. Elijah evidenced it when he faced the prophets of Baal on Carmel. Job showed it when he was covered with boils and surrounded by misunderstanding. Moses used it when he stood against Pharaoh and refused to be intimidated. The fact is, it's impossible to live victoriously for Christ without courage. That's why

God's thrice spoken command to Joshua is as timeless as it is true: "Be strong and courageous!" (Josh. 1:6, 7, 9).

Are you? Honestly now—are you? Or are you quick to quit . . . ready to run when the heat rises? Let it be remembered that real courage is not limited to the battlefield or the Indianapolis 500 or bravely catching a thief in your house. The real tests of courage are much broader . . . much deeper . . . much quieter. They are the inner tests, like remaining faithful when nobody's looking . . . like enduring pain when the room is empty . . . like standing alone when you're misunderstood.

You will never be asked to share your attic with a rattler. But every day, in some way, your courage will be tested. Your tests may not be as exciting as a beachhead landing or sailing around Cape Horn or a space walk. It may be as simple as saying no, as uneventful as facing a pile of dirty laundry, or as unknown as a struggle within yourself between right and wrong. God's Medal of Honor winners are made in secret because their most courageous acts occur down deep inside . . . away from the hurricane of public opinion . . . up in the attic, hidden from public knowledge.[8]

How easy life would be if we knew the future, if we were aware of the outcome of every step before we took it! Life isn't like that, though, and there's a reason for it. God wants you to grow in faith and to trust Him completely. Courage is a prerequisite for a successful life that God blesses. In Christ we can have courage and move forward to be all He intends us to be.

Digging Deeper: Make Your Decision

Is there a decision that you need to make? Are you trying to decide what school to go to, what job to take, where to live, whether you should marry the person you have been dating? Whatever decision you are facing, take some time right now to apply the principles you have learned in this book.

Take your journal and go to a quiet spot, a place where you can be alone, think, and pray about the decision you need to make.

Think about the six principles in this chapter:

- *The Need for Peace.* As you consider the decision you are leaning toward, do you feel peace?
- *The Need for God's Perfect Timing.* A good rule of thumb is to list the reasons that this is the best time to make your decision.
- *The Need for Rest.* One of the very best things you can do before you say yes or no to a major decision is to take some time alone and rest with God.
- *The Need for Resolve.* Ask yourself, *Am I neutral concerning this decision? Am I open to whatever might occur once the decision is made? Do I desire God's outcome and not my own?*
- *The Need for Wisdom.* Listen for God's voice. Consider the desires or burdens He has placed on your heart. Pray for God's confirmation. Step out in faith. Look for open and closed doors of providence.
- *The Need for Courage.* Many decisions require that you take the initiative to move forward.

Once you have spent some time reviewing the above key principles, spend a little more time and apply Mueller's method to your decision-making process:

- First, surrender your will.
- Second, seek the Spirit's will through God's Word.
- Third, note providential circumstances.
- Fourth, pray for guidance.
- Fifth, wait on God.

If you are diligent in seeking God's will in the decision you must make, you are sure to find the right answer, the right path, and the right choice.

"So be strong and take courage, all you who put your hope in the LORD!" (Ps. 31:24 NLT).

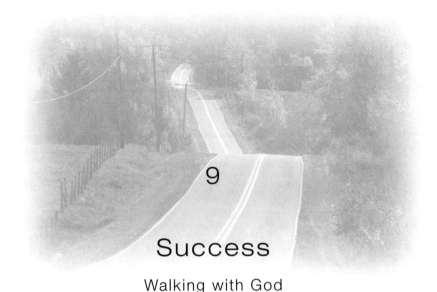

9

Success

Walking with God

In 1923, a group of the world's most successful financiers met at a Chicago hotel. Among those present were the president of the largest independent steel company in the world, the president of the largest utility company, the most successful commodity speculator, the president of the New York Stock Exchange, the president of the Bank of International Settlements, and the head of the world's greatest monopoly at that time.

Together these tycoons of the business world controlled more wealth than the treasury of the United States (remember that we were on the gold standard at that time). For years the media had been printing and talking about the success stories of these wealthy men. They had been held up as examples for all to follow, especially the youth of our nation. These men were at the very pinnacle of success in their world.

Let's take another look and see what happened to these men twenty-five years later.

Charles Schwab was the president of the largest independent steel company in the world. Twenty-five years later, he was living on borrowed money for the last five years of his life and died penniless. Incidentally, he was the first man in American history to draw an annual salary of one million dollars.

Arthur Cutten, the greatest and most successful of commodity speculators, died abroad in dire poverty.

Richard Whitney, the president of the New York Stock Exchange, was sentenced to serve a term in Sing Sing Prison.

Albert Fall, who was a member of the president's cabinet, was pardoned from prison so he could die at home.

Leon Fraser, president of the Bank of International Settlement, ended his life by committing suicide.

All of these men, considered at one time the very epitome of success, had learned how to make money—and lots of it. But in the final analysis, not one of them had really learned how to live. Life is much more than accumulating riches or material things.[1]

If these powerful men did not paint an accurate picture of success, who can? These men all learned how to make money and capture attractive positions but failed in knowing how to live life successfully.

What is true success, anyway? It's living in such a way that you are using what God has given you—your intellect, abilities, gifts, and energy—to accomplish the purpose He intends for your life.

In short, success is doing God's will.

I press on toward the goal to win the prize for which God has called me heavenward in Christ Jesus.

Philippians 3:14 NIV

THE PURPOSE OF THIS BOOK has been to give you guidelines that will help you determine the will of God for your life. I am convinced that the only way to find true fulfillment and happiness in life is to align your life with the will of the Creator. Furthermore, because God created us, only He can fulfill the purpose for which we were brought into being. My hope is that you will join hands with God and say, "Thy will be done," to experience His plan for your life. This is true success.

In this final chapter, allow me to impart some wisdom that may help you on the road to a successful life. The golden nuggets you're about to read can sustain and encourage you on the long road of life. Because the will of God encompasses your entire life, the principles contained in this chapter focus on your long-term walk with God rather than on short-term remedies.

Keep On

"And let us run with endurance the race that God has set before us" (Heb. 12:1 NLT).

The following is said of the legendary Welch preacher D. Martyn Lloyd-Jones, who was admired by many.

One day a young, aspiring preacher decided to pay him a visit. After the service, this young man decided he would follow the older preacher to the back of the church to see what this incredible man of God had to say to people as they shook his hand at the door. Perhaps he thought he could gain some amazing insight into the preacher's success. So, he took his place next to the old man and began listening. What he heard shocked him. The old preacher simply said one thing to each person as they shook his hand at the door: "Keep on!"[2]

One by one, each church member was told the same thing: "Keep on."

The young preacher was disappointed and puzzled. Was "Keep on" the only thing this legendary preacher had to say to his people? But as he pondered the matter in the days and weeks ahead, it occurred to him that those two words—"Keep on"—were, in fact, quite remarkable. Why was that phrase so remarkable? Because it states one of the single most important keys to a successful life: to continue walking with God daily. Getting sidetracked and succumbing to the temptation to compromise is one of the greatest threats to success. The old preacher had learned this wisdom and joyfully passed it along to his flock.

How does one "keep on" with Christ? In a single word: commitment.

Never give up. Again I say, never give up! At times the Christian life requires tenacity, fortitude, and determination. The great apostle Paul said it best in his letter to the Philippian church.

> I do not mean that I am already as God wants me to be. I have not yet reached that goal, but I continue trying to reach it and to make it mine. Christ wants me to do that, which is the reason he made me his. Brothers and sisters, I know that I have not yet reached that goal, but there is one thing I always do. Forgetting the past and straining toward what

174

is ahead, I keep trying to reach the goal and get the prize for which God called me through Christ to the life above. All of us who are spiritually mature should think this way, too. And if there are things you do not agree with, God will make them clear to you.

Philippians 3:12–15 NCV

There will be times in life when you will be tempted to throw all that you have in Christ into the wind. At times the temptation will be strong. Therefore, you must have the resolve to keep on! There will be times of doubt when things do not go your way, and times when it seems God does not hear your prayers. There will be times when you feel like you are swimming against the tide of life, even while trying to accomplish things for God; there will be times of failure. God doesn't necessarily make the road of life easy for His children. But He does guarantee that the road He leads you on will make you more like Him.

Keep venturing out in faith. You may have to fight a battle more than once to win it, and you may have to strengthen your sense of commitment, but it will all be worthwhile in the end, and God will honor you for your steadfastness, patience, and endurance.

One athlete sums up the urgency of keeping on.

When David Yudovin entered the chilly 64-degree water before dawn, he was trying to complete a journey he had begun nearly 20 years before. In 1978, only 250 yards from the end of a marathon swim near Ventura, California, Yudovin had a near-fatal heart attack. He fought his way back to health and later completed several landmark swims. Now, at age 45, he felt ready to take on his supreme challenge, swimming the English Channel.

The odds against a successful channel swim are great. Yudovin had tried three times before and failed. The lure of that 21-plus mile stretch of icy water never left him, though. The swim would be dangerous, not only because of the frigid

175

water, but because the channel was often laced with sewage, oil slicks, seaweed, jellyfish, and up to 400 ships a day. On August 20, 1996, the weather reports indicated it was now or never for Yudovin, so he swam. Eight hours into the swim, a storm cell arrived, producing hard rain, strong tidal flow, and extremely choppy water. But Yudovin continued on. And when he climbed out of the cold water near Calais, France, he was elated. "It's so rewarding and so fulfilling it almost tickles inside," he said. His fourth attempt was a victory![3]

The secret to having the determination to pursue God's will is found in two things. First, it's in what fuels you. If you believe with all your heart that Christ and the Word of God are the greatest things on earth—the ultimate truth, the most wonderful way of life, the only path to true fulfillment, and the only road to life eternal—then you have the right fuel. As you continue with Christ, He will bring you through new experiences that will answer your big questions and give you unshakable faith.

The second part of the secret is the dynamite power of the Holy Spirit in your life, power that will give you inner spiritual strength and guidance so you can walk hand in hand with God into a successful future.

The Bible says: "But when the Holy Spirit comes to you, you will receive power. You will be my witnesses—in Jerusalem, in all of Judea, in Samaria, and in every part of the world" (Acts 1:8 NCV).

The road of life will have many unexpected curves and surprises. But life will be a success if you can persist in running the race with God. Martyn Lloyd-Jones understood one of the most important truths to be communicated to his congregation. If they would just continue on with Christ, everything would fall into place. "Show me the path where I should walk, O LORD; point out the right road for me to follow" (Ps. 25:4 NLT).

Donald Grey Barnhouse retells a story that the philosopher Cervantes once told:

> The road is always better than the inn. . . . There is a road, a lone traveler and, at the edge of the horizon, an inn toward which the traveler is hurrying as fast as he can, oblivious of where he is and what there is to see about him. He has a goal to reach and to reach that goal he misses the profits and blessings possible to him on the journey.

Barnhouse comments:

> It is the way we hurry through life. We set up goals like inns and hurry and struggle and toil to get them achieved. We hurry to get the home paid off, the retirement account stocked full, the children to grow up and retirement to come. But all the while as we hurry down the road to achieve these goals and get to these inns, we are missing life. We never learn how to live. In our haste to live life and acquire personal gain, we pass life itself and the profits of enjoying its splendor. We miss the blessings of God on the road, failing to see those we might help, the beauty as we pass, and the very purpose of our existence. We need the endurance of patience to have a life well lived.[4]

Growing with God is a daily event. It is personal and exclusive. Sometimes the road with God is blessed and enjoyable, while at other times you must be patient and endure difficult times. We have all heard the words "Bloom where you are planted." Yet more often than not, we bristle at the thought of doing it. Oh, for the grace to rejoice in all circumstances, knowing God is at work—for His good and ours!

> Jockeys who consistently ride into the winner's circle are in complete control of their horses when they race. The winning horse is referred to as the "meekest on the track." Why? Because a winning horse responds quickly to the jockey's

commands and is totally submitted to its rider. On the other hand, self-willed and fractious horses frequently are left at the gate. And even though they may run faster than the others, they make mistakes and rarely finish among the leaders.

This understanding of meekness on the horse track is related to an ancient definition of meekness: "yielding the will to the bit and the bridle."

If we willingly yield our lives to God—to the "bit and the bridle" of His will—then we are in the best position to win life's race.[5]

Jesus said, "Blessed are the meek, for they shall inherit the earth" (Matt. 5:5).

Being happy in life comes with the understanding that God's will is tailor-made for each person, including you. God has a custom-made plan designed just for you. Consider His providence—the fact that He is always at work in your life and that He guides your destiny. That should bring you great peace. Indeed, God's ever-present guidance brings us mental comfort and encouragement, even in times when it seems He may have forgotten us.

Remember that Jesus Christ commanded you to live for the day and not to worry: "Don't worry and say, 'What will we eat?' or 'What will we drink?' or 'What will we wear?' . . . The thing you should want most is God's kingdom and doing what God wants. Then all these other things you need will be given to you. So don't worry about tomorrow, because tomorrow will have its own worries. Each day has enough trouble of its own" (Matt. 6:31, 33–34 NCV).

Are you running down the path of life in a rush to get to the next goal? Slow down. Seize the moment. Stop and smell the roses. Life is short and God desires for you to live for today. Practically speaking, take some time alone each day to meet with God in prayer and speak to Him about your life. As you are performing your daily routine, slow down to observe life and consider what God would want you to do. You will find that very often, right in the midst of your present circumstances, God is speaking to you and His will is unfolding.

God's Will and Yours

"Truly, O God of Israel, our Savior, you work in strange and mysterious ways" (Isa. 45:15 NLT). God's will is often a big surprise to us when He makes it known. What you are least likely to expect in life can sometimes be the very will of God for you. Here is an example from the life of Chuck Swindoll. When he was in eighth grade, all Chuck Swindoll wanted for Christmas was a new basketball. His father, who worked in a machine shop, had made him an iron hoop for a basket. Chuck practiced until he could sink nine out of ten free throws, and he worked hard on a two-hand set throw.

Then one November evening, his old tattered basketball burst. With six weeks to go before Christmas, he dropped numerous hints and did his chores with renewed energy, even volunteering to wax the kitchen floor! Sure enough, a brightly wrapped box appeared under the Christmas tree—the right shape, the right sound when shaken, and with Chuck's name written on it. He could hardly wait. On Christmas Day, he tore at the wrapping only to discover a world globe inside. It had no bounce to it.

Disappointed at the time, Chuck has reflected back on this experience: "My mother's vision eclipsed my fantasy and became my reality. I still enjoy watching basketball, but what really excites me is the idea of sharing our Savior with people in places like Singapore and Moscow, Delhi and Montreal."[6] What are your dreams? Are they God's dreams?

God's will for your life is a completely individualistic issue. Never fall into the trap of believing that you are like everybody else on the planet. You are not. God has made you unique and there is nobody like you in history. Scientists are proving this through genetic research. Consider the way in which He has made you—your God-given abilities and desires, your personality, your strengths, and your weaknesses. Your life is complex and special, but God understands it completely, and this should encourage you to seek His will for you.

Pay attention to God's leading in your life. Learn to listen to Him and His Word. This takes time and patience. There is no established pattern for His leading or method for our seeking it. There are biblical principles to understanding God's leading, which we have covered in this book, but God will not be placed in a box. His ways are mysterious. He wants us to glory in Him and glorify His name. And you will find that God does lead you, even when you cannot understand the way.

Consider the following story.

> A woman in Alaska tried to call her sister in Idaho, but mistakenly dialed a house in Vermont. She got through to 89-year-old Mildred Connor, who, at that moment, was suffering a severe heart attack. At that point, the Alaskan woman heard a gasping voice with weak breath saying, "Help me—help me. Please, God, help me."
>
> Alice Witt meant to call Area Code 208, but called 802 instead and reached Rutland, Vermont. She and her husband were able to work with telephone operators and emergency personnel, who rushed to the scene and saved Mildred Connor's life.
>
> Sometimes when I pray I think all I get are busy signals or wrong numbers. But God is working in ways that, if I'll just hang in there, time will prove over and over again His hand throughout.[7]

God's will often entails hidden surprises. On the other hand, many people have experienced His will in very practical ways. They have an innate understanding of what God wants and follow the doors that open along life's path. Mastering the art of knowing the will of God takes time, focus, and dedication. Be open to the process and willing to receive God's will no matter what it may turn out to be.

As you seek God's will, allow Paul's praise of God in Ephesians to be a source of encouragement to you: "Now glory be to God! By his mighty power at work within us, he is able to accomplish infinitely more than we would ever dare to ask or hope" (Eph. 3:20 NLT). The Greek word translated *power* in this verse is the root word for our English word *dynamite*. God's dynamite power is able to do all things in your life. As you journey out in faith, count on the fact that God is directing you and is present in your life, because He desires to do His will through you. As you leave the future up to Him, you will be pleasantly surprised at the results. I hope you will take this promise to heart and make it your own.

Right and Wrong Decisions

"He makes my feet like hinds' feet, and sets me upon my high places" (Ps. 18:33 NASB). Some people are surprised when they find that people who pray for God's direction in life can actually make wrong decisions. But, of course, it is true. That's why it is so important to pray that God will help us in our ignorance—much as he helps the hind walk on cliffs. With our old sinful nature waging war against us, it can be easy to make a mess of things.

I am reminded of a story about a young man who was the youngest executive in a new firm. He saw the president of the firm eating lunch in the lunchroom one day and decided to hazard a visit and ask some questions that might score him some points. He sat across from the president of the company, and as they were eating, he asked, "Sir, how can I be successful?" The president paused for a moment from his sandwich, looked up, and said, "Work hard." The young man went on, "Yes, sir, but how do I work hard?" The president looked up again briefly and said, "Make good decisions." The young man went on, "How do I make good decisions?" The president responded, "Learn by experience." To which the young man finally said, "What experience?" The president, slightly aggravated by this young man's persistence, paused and turned to the young man and looking him straight in the eyes said "Making bad decisions."

We should strive to learn how to make good decisions in life. Certainly, we will fail from time to time, but we need to learn from those failures. Good decision making is an art. It requires the knowledge of God's Word and the ability to discern His leading.

When you find that you have made a wrong turn, it is vital to change course and get back on the right track. Several good rules of thumb apply in turning around a bad decision:

1. Admit your failure.
2. Clean up any mess you have created (ask forgiveness if necessary).
3. Follow through with commitments that should not be broken.
4. Go to God in prayer for spiritual refreshment.
5. Get God's new direction.
6. Move out with God's power.

Remember, wrong decisions are not the end of the world. Everyone makes them from time to time. In the end, wrong decisions made by a person who really loves and lives for God will work out for good, but we may have to go through some difficult times before they do. "And we know that in all things God works for the good of those who love him, who have been called according to his purpose" (Rom. 8:28 NIV).

Follow-up and Follow-through

When you make a successful decision in life, your natural inclination may be to bask in the glory of the success, but prudence and God's Word dictate otherwise. *Follow-up* means that you take the success and plan how you will sustain it, motivate the people around you by it, glorify God through it, and seek His wisdom concerning your future steps.

Following through on success requires that you complete the work you have begun, reward the people who helped you get there, show meekness and integrity, and do not let success go to your head or sidetrack you. Guard against pride, which can leave you wide open to defeat, despite your recent success.

One of the greatest traps for Christians is prosperity. Many have experienced success in life only to forget God and misuse the very success He has granted. They end up failing miserably. Indeed, the sidelines of God's kingdom are lined with people who have disqualified themselves from a true victory because they exchanged their walk with God for worldly riches and success. When things go right for you, the proper response is to give all the glory to God and thank Him for everything.

Leave a Legacy

"He [God] commanded our ancestors to teach [His laws and decrees] to their children, so the next generation might know them—even the children not yet born—that they in turn might teach their children. So each generation can set its hope anew on God, remembering his glorious miracles and obeying his commands" (Ps. 78:5–7 NLT).

Those who have experienced God's work in their lives are able to leave a godly legacy. You can have wealth, but if you do not have wisdom, the wealth will be squandered. You can bequeath your home and estate to others, but if you do not leave the memory of a life lived for God, the material inheritance has little value. Leaving a godly legacy means that you are giving your faith to others, making new disciples, and building into their lives the principles of Christ that will be carried on for generations to come. To put it simply, leaving such a legacy is true success.

One person who left a powerful legacy in my life was a man known as Uncle Jim.

When I was about thirteen years old, my best friend, Dave, invited me on a camping trip with his Uncle Jim. We camped at the beach where, at night, Uncle Jim would spend time playing chess with me. He surprised me by telling me about Jesus Christ during our chess game. He did so in a very masterful way, asking me simple and sometimes profound questions about life. Often in his answers he would talk about God. I was sincerely interested in his words because he was sincerely interested in me. Later I found out that he was a very well-known high school principal who was deeply loved by his students. I will never forget that first trip with Uncle Jim. I was greatly impressed by his statements about God, even though I was undergoing the many worldly changes and temptations that often accompany the teenage years.

A year or so later we took our second camping trip to the High Sierras in central California. I looked forward to being with Uncle Jim again, and this time he promised to take us kids backpacking five miles into the inner lake region of the beautiful Sierra Mountains. I had never been backpacking before, so I was excited.

On this trip with Uncle Jim, I would not hear about Jesus, but I would see a sermon.

We broke camp at the foot of the mountains and began up the trail in the afternoon. But what was supposed to be a two-hour hike ended up taking five hours. We hiked through streams and trails in the dark of night. All four of us kids began hearing things in the woods. We thought they were bears. We were incredibly scared. Uncle Jim kept us together. At about 9:00 p.m. we arrived at the campsite. The next day he took us fishing. This was an unforgettable experience.

It was on the way up the trail, however, that I learned something that has stayed with me to this day. As we were trekking behind Uncle Jim, I noticed something about him that seemed different. His hair. He had lost a great deal since the last time I had seen him. It had turned gray. He seemed so much older. I asked Dave about it as we were walking together up the switchbacks, and he told me sadly that Uncle Jim had cancer "pretty bad."

Shocked, I asked, "Will he die?"

And Dave said, "Yes." Here was a man in his forties with cancer taking a group of young boys up a mountain. I thought of Christ.

Not long after that, the cancer took its toll and Uncle Jim died. It was at his funeral that I would receive the most lasting witness. For I had never in my life attended a funeral where hundreds and hundreds of people turned out to celebrate a life well lived. Person after person gave testimony to the life of a man who had influenced so many for the kingdom of God. It was a joyful and tearful occasion. Years later when I finally committed my life to Christ, Uncle Jim was one of the people to whom I attributed my conversion. Uncle Jim left a legacy.

What type of legacy will you leave? Whose life are you influencing? Are you having an impact on the minds of your children, your wife or husband, family, friends, neighbors? All are important. Think about all that you are building into these people's lives. The question is, What are you building? Begin establishing your legacy today. The method is simple—communicate Christ with your lips and your life.

Integrity

The Scriptures encourage you to live a life of integrity, which results in a blessed assurance of God's presence with you. Many people and families today have been destroyed because of a lack of integrity. However, when a person decides to turn his or her life around, restoration can begin. Job 8:6 says: "If you are pure and live with complete integrity, he will rise up and restore your happy home" (NLT).

The same holds true for a business and a nation. God is in the restoration business and can work miracles as you walk with Him. There is also security for those who desire to walk with integrity. Psalm 37:25 says: "Once I was young, and now I am old. Yet I have never seen the godly forsaken, nor seen their children begging for bread" (NLT).

In this life you may never have an opportunity to preach a sermon in a church, but you will have many opportunities to shine forth the light of Christ as you witness to hundreds through your daily life and example. It's true that your reputation—not your words—will follow you to the grave.

The proceedings of the U.S. Naval Institute tell a tremendous story of the power of integrity at work.

The USS *Astoria* (CA-34) was the first U.S. cruiser to engage the Japanese during the Battle of Savo Island, a night action fought 8–9 August 1942. Although she scored two hits on the Imperial flagship *Chokai*, the *Astoria* was badly damaged and sank shortly after noon, 9 August.

About 0200 hours a young Midwesterner, Signalman 3rd Class Elgin Staples, was swept overboard by the blast when the *Astoria's* number one eight-inch gun turret exploded. Wounded in both legs by shrapnel and in semi-shock, he was kept afloat by a narrow lifebelt that he managed to activate with a simple trigger mechanism.

At around 0600 hours, Staples was rescued by a passing destroyer and returned to the *Astoria*, whose captain was attempting to save the cruiser by beaching her. The effort failed, and Staples, still wearing the same lifebelt, found himself back in the water. It was lunchtime. Picked up again, this time by the USS *President Jackson* (AP-37), he was one of 500 survivors of the battle who were evacuated to Noumea.

On board the transport Staples, for the first time, closely examined the lifebelt that had served him so well. It had been manufactured by Firestone Tire and Rubber Company of Akron, Ohio, and bore a registration number.

Given home leave Staples told his story and asked his mother, who worked for Firestone, about the purpose of the number on the belt. She replied that the company insisted on personal responsibility for the war effort, and that the number was unique and assigned to only one inspector. Staples remembered everything about the lifebelt, and quoted the number. It was his mother's personal code and affixed to every item she was responsible for approving.[8]*

David Jeremiah comments on this story:

Fifty years ago, a mother's unheralded integrity in an anonymous wartime job made sure her soon-to-be shipwrecked son's hope of survival. But how much greater are the stakes in eternal matters, and how much greater is the challenge to diligence in eternal matters![9]

Historians tell us one of the reasons America became such a great country has to do with the work ethic brought here by Europeans after the Reformation period. They instilled in the colonists the goal to do all things for the glory of Christ. Quality, honesty, professionalism, and solid commitments marked their trades and professions and thus produced American products that were unrivaled. It is clear today that we have lost this work ethic. For example, today one of the greatest sources of loss in American

*Reprinted from *Proceedings* with permission from the U.S. Naval Institute.

business is employee theft, totaling more than one billion dollars per year.

Though our society teaches that a title or a college degree is what determines a person's success, in reality character and commitment to living for God are more important. People may listen to your words because of your position or title, but if you don't follow through on your commitments, they will soon begin to ignore you.

In all of life exhibit integrity, so that it will be your legacy. When we commit the work of our hands to Christ, we are a witness here on earth to His lordship. As others see the beauty of a job well done, we may have the opportunity to speak the gospel and save lives.

Ephesians 4:13 says: "We must become like a mature person, growing until we become like Christ and have his perfection" (NCV). Our personal growth and maturity, both as Christians and as responsible human beings, are the most important aspects of success. The closer you walk with God on the road of life, the more you will grow and mature in the faith. It is important to remember that you are a work in progress. God has begun a good work in you, but it will not be finished until you go to be with Him. Success in following the will of God is a lifelong process.

Our greatest growth is often realized as we journey with God on the hot, dusty road of life, experiencing the trials and tribulations that come our way. On this road God bids us to come close to Him, to rely on His Word, and to trust Him even when the way seems dark. Our character is best shaped while we are trudging the hills and valleys of life's journey. As we grow in Him, He is able to put us on the high roads of blessing, where we learn to keep our feet on the ground and handle the greatest of all temptations—promotion and prosperity—while giving glory to Him. When we learn to follow God's direction, regardless of the difficult landscape through which we must pass, we enjoy His blessings and gracefully bear fruit for His kingdom on our way.

A number of years ago the most magnificent diamond in the history of the world was found in an African mine. It was then presented to the king of England to embellish his crown of state. The king sent it to Amsterdam to be cut by an expert stonecutter. Can you imagine what he did with it?

He took this gem of priceless value and cut a notch in it. Then he struck it hard one time with his hammer, and the majestic jewel fell into his hand, broken in two. What recklessness! What wastefulness! What criminal carelessness!

Actually, that was not the case at all. For you see, the one blow with the hammer had been studied and planned for days, and even weeks. Drawings and models had been made of the gem. Its quality, defects, and possible lines along which it could split had all been studied to the smallest detail. And the man to whom it was entrusted was one of the most skilled stonecutters in all the world.

Now, do you believe that blow was a mistake? No, it was the capstone and culmination of the stonecutter's skill. When he struck that blow, he did the one thing that would bring that gem to its most perfect shape, radiance, and jeweled splendor. The blow that seemed to be the ruin of the majestic stone was actually its perfect redemption, for from the halves were fashioned two magnificent gems. Only the skilled eye of the expert stonecutter could have seen the beauty of two diamonds hidden in the rough, uncut stone as it came from the mine.

Sometimes, in the same way, God lets a stinging blow fall on your life. You bleed, feeling the pain, and your soul cries out in agony. At first you think the blow is an appalling mistake. But it is not, for you are the most precious jewel in the world to God. And He is the most skilled stonecutter in the universe.

Someday you are to be a jewel adorning the crown of the King. As you lie in His hand now, He knows just how to deal with you. Not one blow will be permitted to fall on your apprehensive soul except what the love of God allows.

And you may be assured that from the depths of the experience, you will see untold blessings and spiritual enrichment like you have never known before.

In a George MacDonald book, one of the characters makes this bitter statement: "I wonder why God made me. I certainly don't see any purpose in it!" Another character responds, "Perhaps you don't see any purpose yet, but then, He isn't finished making you. And besides, you are arguing with the process."

If people would only believe they are still in the process of creation, submit to the Maker, allow Him to handle them as the potter handles clay, and yield themselves in one shining, deliberate action to the turning of His wheel, they would soon find themselves able to welcome every pressure from His hand on them, even if it results in pain. And sometimes they should not only believe but also have God's purpose in sight: "bringing many sons to glory" (Heb. 2:10).[10]

Why does God work in this way? Because if you are not mature enough to handle God's gifts and blessings, you will most certainly make a mess of them. Our world's present condition bears witness to this. The power brokers of our day are unprepared to manage because many of them do not know God. Only God who created all things can prepare a person to manage those things.

As you go through the difficulties of life, you will learn tremendous truths about yourself that will help you change and mature. This maturing process is an enormous part of being a Christian yet is missing in the world. The world is filled with people who have never grown up, people who reject God's moral truth and become entrapped in sinful habits, such as a prideful attitude that refuses to yield to others; selfish desires to be right, first, and best; short-tempered, quick-fused reactions to others; greed for material gain; and the lust for pleasure, jealousy, and gossip. These habits of the world stunt the growth of people and cause misery. Yes, sinful habits can destroy our lives and the lives of those around us.

Resolving to change the bad habits that ensnare us and make us miserable is the quickest road to recovery and happiness. When we resolve in our hearts to face who we are in the light of God's Word and allow Christ to change us, the result is happiness and peace. Marriages and families are restored, relationships are healed, finances are put in balance, children are cared for, and work is done with integrity. The list of blessings that can result from one person's turning his or her life over to Christ is endless. Christ matures us and brings us into the proper balance of life for which He created us.

God's Word reveals much about our sin nature, and His Spirit gives us the power to make the changes needed so that we can be more Christlike. When we follow God's program, we will mature in faith. When we commit ourselves to Christ and learn to live according to His Word, we will experience true happiness.

The purity of our lives is of paramount importance, because the best sermon is the life that is lived faithfully in public and private. There can be no substitute for a holy life. Live by the principles of God's Word and for His glory, and you will not be ashamed.

Finishing Well

"Remember that in a race everyone runs, but only one person gets the prize. You also must run in such a way that you will win" (1 Cor. 9:24 NLT). Paul was keenly aware of the brevity of time and the importance of finishing life well. Toward the end of his life when he knew the death sentence from Rome was imminent, he wrote Timothy, a young protégé whom he had installed as the pastor of the church in the ancient Roman city of Ephesus. Paul wrote these words to Timothy:

I charge you therefore before God and the Lord Jesus Christ, who will judge the living and the dead at His appearing and

His kingdom: Preach the word! Be ready in season and out of season. Convince, rebuke, exhort, with all longsuffering and teaching. For the time will come when they will not endure sound doctrine, but according to their own desires, because they have itching ears, they will heap up for themselves teachers; and they will turn their ears away from the truth, and be turned aside to fables. But you be watchful in all things, endure afflictions, do the work of an evangelist, fulfill your ministry. For I am already being poured out as a drink offering, and the time of my departure is at hand. I have fought the good fight, I have finished the race, I have kept the faith. Finally, there is laid up for me the crown of righteousness, which the Lord, the righteous Judge, will give to me on that Day, and not to me only but also to all who have loved His appearing.

2 Timothy 4:1–8

Paul encouraged his disciple to continue to perform the work God had called him to do. "Fulfill your ministry," he said. What is the ministry to which God has called you? Perhaps you are keenly aware of it; possibly, you are not. But in time, if you are walking closely with Christ, you will know what He is calling you to do.

The apostle also encouraged Timothy by example. He said, "I have fought the good fight, I have finished the race." Paul likened the Christian life to a long-distance run in which he would cross the finish line successfully. Paul left this example not only to Timothy but to us as well.

Finally, Paul explained his motivation for finishing well: "Finally, there is laid up for me the crown of righteousness, which the Lord, the righteous Judge, will give to me on that Day, and not to me only but also to all who have loved His appearing." Everyone who has loved Christ and lived for Him will receive the crown of righteousness. This is so ironic in a world where unrighteousness seems to rule the day and where a person who desires to live a holy life is often shunned and persecuted. But in the end, when Christ returns and the truth is shown to the whole world, those who have lived for Him will be rewarded. Trust this biblical fact and live for Christ today. Finish your life in faith, purity, and holiness—and set your sights on the crown of righteousness that awaits you.

By nature we are procrastinators. We figure out the future when we get there. But there is room in the will of God for deep thoughtfulness and consideration about the future. What will we do when we retire? Will we retire? How will we serve God? How will we care for our families and grandchildren? To live thoughtfully for Christ, there is a great deal to consider. Though our future is somewhat unpredictable, we should still consider these things in our plan to finish well.

Jesus's final words on the cross were "It is finished." He completed the work the Father had given Him to do—to die for the sins of all humankind. The result of His completed commitment is your salvation and entrance into heaven.

We too have work to do for God. Let us be about that work.

The Results of Doing God's Will

As we have seen, living in God's will should be the goal of every Christian. This is how God designed us, and it is the only way we can be all He wants us to be. As we commit ourselves to doing God's will, we experience true satisfaction, total peace, and eternal fruit.

True Satisfaction

When it comes right down to the bottom line, we all just want to be happy. It is as simple as that. However, doing what you like, being with whom you like, and living where you like will never give you true happiness. Through experience I have found that no matter what I gain in this life that may be of worldly value, it does not fulfill my longings, because fulfillment cannot be found in worldly treasures. Instead, knowing and worshiping our Creator and being in the center of His will brings true fulfillment. "Carry out my instructions; don't forsake them. Guard them, for they will lead you to a fulfilled life" (Prov. 4:13 NLT).

From God's vantage point, success does not mean more money, possessions, or power. Many who experience joy in their relationship with God live in nations of the world where the prosperity of the West is simply not available. God knows our situation and meets us there, providing food for the poor and humility for the wealthy who seek Him.

Total Peace

Jesus taught that the blessing of God's kingdom is personal peace. John 14:27 says: "I leave you peace; my peace I give you. I do not give it to you as the world does. So don't let your hearts be troubled or afraid" (NCV). True success, as defined by God, brings peace in your life. This peace is given to you by God's Spirit and comes through the knowledge of God's Word. It is a peace that surpasses understanding.

As you spend time with the Lord daily through prayer and Bible reading, you will experience His peace. The opposite can be true as well. The less time you spend with God (in prayer, fellowship, and His Word), the less peace you will have. Even in times of difficulty and tragedy, when you lean on the One whose burden is light and yoke is easy, you can know His peace.

The first step to lasting peace is turning your life over to the Prince of Peace, who will transform your heart and infuse your soul with a quiet confidence by the authority and power of His Spirit.

The world clamors for peace on every level yet never finds it. When we are committed to an intimate relationship with Christ and pursue the goals in life that God has given us for His kingdom and not for our own pleasure, we will experience His peace. Knowing that you are in His divine will gives you assurance in every facet of life.

Eternal Fruit

When you plug your life into God's will, the results are always awesome. God wants to use your life for His good to bring forth fruit for His kingdom. This fruit will bless you and those around you.

As you endeavor to do what God leads you to do, even the most basic decisions of life are blessed with powerful results. Such decisions may include a car purchase, buying or selling a home, or a career change—God can use them all for His eternal purposes. These decisions may bring you into new relationships with people whom you touch with God's love, leading them into His kingdom. As you join hands with the Creator, the new relationship, career move, or venture of faith will be used for His glory. Watch and see!

God has a way of miraculously fulfilling His will and your desires at the same time. It's a win-win situation. And Christ promises that when you walk in His will, you will produce the fruits of success. "But when the Holy Spirit controls our lives, he will produce this kind of fruit in us: love, joy, peace, patience, kindness, goodness, faithfulness, gentleness, and self-control" (Gal. 5:22–23 NLT).

God wants to bless your life and use you for good. The principles of God's will, found in His Word, are the pathway to success for your life. "My child, do not forget my teaching, but keep my commands in mind. Then you will live a long time, and your life will be successful" (Prov. 3:1–2 NCV).

Final Thoughts

Clearly the will of God can be one of the most difficult topics to discuss. At the most, we can grasp only the basic biblical principles to knowing His will, which I hope we've covered thoroughly enough in the chapters of this book.

God's ways are wonderful and mysterious. I love this fact about the will of God, because in the end He always surprises me. Therefore, don't ask God for what you think is good; rather, ask Him for what *He thinks is good*. Let God bring to pass an incredible work in you—one that's beyond your wildest imagination.

Each of us desires to have a fulfilling, exciting, storybook life. Yet for most of us, the road of life has many detours and potholes as well as breathtaking scenic routes and refreshing vacation spots. The purpose of this book has been to tell you that God is the one who made you and can lead you through the mysterious path that is your life. But He has given you a choice: You can choose to give your life over to Him, or you can plan it yourself and go it alone.

No matter where the road of life may lead you, God's Word promises that He will always be by your side (see Ps. 18:35; Isa. 58:11). Only when we invite the Giver of life to lead us does life become what it was meant to be, so place your life in the hands of Christ today and allow Him to carry you through many awesome adventures.

Digging Deeper: Recall His Faithfulness

I encourage you to write your major decisions in your journal. Write down the great things you have learned from God and keep them for future reference. Record your failures and accompanying struggles. These valuable memories will help you recall how God has miraculously worked in the past, and they will give you hope for the future.

Finally, think and pray about the following:

196

- *Learn from your decisions.* You are going to make major decisions in the years ahead. Some will change your life for the better, others for the worse. Therefore, it is important that you become wise in the art of decision making and learn to apply the biblical principles for your growth.
- *Develop a new focus in life.* Remember, your goal is not to get God to join your program and bless your plans. Your goal is to join His program for the world and have Him use you in His plan. This is a biblical focus and will result in success if you dedicate your life to be an open and willing vessel for Him.
- *Grow in the knowledge of God's Word.* Clearly the most valuable tool in decision making is the Word of God. Daily meditation and growth in God's Word enables you to be directed for His purposes. Second Timothy 3:16–17 says: "All Scripture is inspired by God and is useful to teach us what is true and to make us realize what is wrong in our lives. It straightens us out and teaches us to do what is right. It is God's way of preparing us in every way, fully equipped for every good thing God wants us to do" (NLT).
- *Grow in the discipline of prayer.* Prayer is two-way communication between you and God. It is often in prayer that your heart will be settled, established, and directed by the Lord.
- *Walk with God in obedience.* A holy and uncompromising walk with God aids you in being open and receptive to His prompting. Psalm 37:23 reads: "The steps of the godly are directed by the LORD. He delights in every detail of their lives" (NLT). It is in this way that you can ensure that in the aftermath of your decisions, God will be with you.
- *Remember that God can use all for good.* It is important for you to understand that God can use your

decisions for good, especially those that have meant failure. In fact, if we're honest with ourselves, we admit that we've all failed at times. God can use failures for good. When you fail, take heart. God is molding you and shaping you into His likeness. Stay with Him, and He will direct your path. "It is not that we think we can do anything of lasting value by ourselves. Our only power and success come from God" (2 Cor. 3:5 NLT).

Bible Reading Schedule

I HAVE PERSONALLY FOUND a reading plan for God's Word to be extremely helpful in the midst of a busy life. It keeps me on track.

As I have mentioned many times in this book, God's Word is a foundation stone for our lives and our divine guidance system. Spending time reading the Bible daily with some focused time in prayer can transform your life. If you are willing, faithful, and courageous to take Him at His word and launch out in faith, you will find that God will bless you and open incredible doors of opportunity.

I recommend beginning your day early with this reading program followed with prayer. Normally, I conclude with the Psalms, reading systematically through them, one each day, and using that one as a prayer for the day. This of course means that I read through the Psalms more than once per year, and it seems that I never tire of them.

If you follow the plan below, you will read through the Bible in one year, or you can create your own reading program so that you are reading the Word of God each day. You may want to read from the Old and New Testaments each day and then conclude with the Psalms. Perhaps you will want to read both in the morning and at night. Be flexible and choose the best program for you. The important thing is to begin and end your day with the Lord. After all, He is the one who created the days and evenings that we might spend them with Him!

January

1 Genesis 1–3
2 Joshua 1–4
3 Job 1–3
4 Ezekiel 1–2
5 Matthew 1–2
6 Romans 1–4
7 Isaiah 1–3
8 Genesis 4–7
9 Joshua 5–8
10 Job 4–7
11 Ezekiel 3–4
12 Matthew 3–4
13 Romans 5–7
14 Isaiah 4–6
15 Genesis 8–10
16 Joshua 9–12
17 Job 8–10
18 Ezekiel 5–6
19 Matthew 5–6
20 Romans 8–10
21 Isaiah 7–9
22 Genesis 11–14
23 Joshua 13–16
24 Job 11–14
25 Ezekiel 7–8
26 Matthew 7–8
27 Romans 11–13
28 Isaiah 10–12
29 Genesis 15–18
30 Joshua 17–20
31 Job 15–18

February

1 Ezekiel 9–10
2 Matthew 9–10
3 Romans 14–16
4 Isaiah 13–15
5 Genesis 19–21
6 Joshua 21–24
7 Job 19–21
8 Ezekiel 11–12
9 Matthew 11–12
10 1 Corinthians 1–4
11 Isaiah 16–18
12 Genesis 22–25
13 Judges 1–5
14 Job 22–26
15 Ezekiel 13–14
16 Matthew 13–14
17 1 Corinthians 5–7
18 Isaiah 19–21
19 Genesis 26–28
20 Judges 6–10
21 Job 27–31
22 Ezekiel 15–16
23 Matthew 15–16
24 1 Corinthians 8–10
25 Isaiah 22–24
26 Genesis 29–31
27 Judges 11–16
28 Job 32–37

March

1 Ezekiel 17–18
2 Matthew 17–18
3 1 Corinthians 11–13
4 Isaiah 25–27
5 Genesis 32–34
6 Judges 17–21
7 Job 38–42
8 Ezekiel 19–20
9 Matthew 19–20
10 1 Corinthians 14–16
11 Isaiah 28–30
12 Genesis 35–37
13 Ruth 1–4
14 Psalms 1–5
15 Ezekiel 21–22
16 Matthew 21–22
17 2 Corinthians 1–3
18 Isaiah 31–33
19 Genesis 38–40
20 1 Samuel 1–5
21 Psalms 6–10
22 Ezekiel 23–24
23 Matthew 23–24
24 2 Corinthians 4–6
25 Isaiah 34–36
26 Genesis 41–43
27 1 Samuel 6–10
28 Psalms 11–15
29 Ezekiel 25–26
30 Matthew 25–26
31 2 Corinthians 7–9

April

1 Isaiah 37–39
2 Genesis 44–46
3 1 Samuel 11–15
4 Psalms 16–20
5 Ezekiel 27–28
6 Matthew 27–28
7 2 Corinthians 10–13
8 Isaiah 40–42
9 Genesis 47–50
10 1 Samuel 16–20
11 Psalms 21–25
12 Ezekiel 29–30
13 Mark 1–2
14 Galatians 1–2
15 Isaiah 43–45
16 Exodus 1–4
17 1 Samuel 21–25
18 Psalms 26–30
19 Ezekiel 31–32
20 Mark 3–4
21 Galatians 3–4
22 Isaiah 46–48

200

23	Exodus 5–8
24	1 Samuel 26–31
25	Psalms 31–35
26	Ezekiel 33–34
27	Mark 5–6
28	Galatians 5–6
29	Isaiah 49–50
30	Exodus 9–12

May

1	2 Samuel 1–5
2	Psalms 36–40
3	Ezekiel 35–36
4	Mark 7–8
5	Ephesians 1–2
6	Isaiah 51–52
7	Exodus 13–16
8	2 Samuel 6–10
9	Psalms 41–45
10	Ezekiel 37–38
11	Mark 9–10
12	Ephesians 3–4
13	Isaiah 53–54
14	Exodus 17–19
15	2 Samuel 11–15
16	Psalms 46–50
17	Ezekiel 39–40
18	Mark 11–12
19	Ephesians 5–6
20	Isaiah 55–56
21	Exodus 20–23
22	2 Samuel 16–20
23	Psalms 51–55
24	Ezekiel 41–42
25	Mark 13–14
26	Philippians 1–2
27	Isaiah 57–58
28	Exodus 24–27
29	2 Samuel 21–24
30	Psalms 56–60
31	Ezekiel 43–44

June

1	Mark 15–16
2	Philippians 3–4
3	Isaiah 59–60
4	Exodus 28–30
5	1 Kings 1–5

6	Psalms 61–65
7	Ezekiel 45–46
8	Luke 1–2
9	Colossians 1–2
10	Isaiah 61–63
11	Exodus 31–34
12	1 Kings 6–10
13	Psalms 66–70
14	Ezekiel 47–48
15	Luke 3–4
16	Colossians 3–4
17	Isaiah 64–66
18	Exodus 35–40
19	1 Kings 11–16
20	Psalms 71–75
21	Daniel 1–2
22	Luke 5–6
23	1 Thessalonians 1–2
24	Jeremiah 1–2
25	Leviticus 1–4
26	1 Kings 17–22
27	Psalms 76–80
28	Daniel 3–4
29	Luke 7–8
30	1 Thessalonians 3–5

July

1	Jeremiah 3–4
2	Leviticus 5–8
3	2 Kings 1–5
4	Psalms 81–85
5	Daniel 5–6
6	Luke 9–10
7	2 Thessalonians 1–3
8	Jeremiah 5–6
9	Leviticus 9–12
10	2 Kings 6–10
11	Psalms 86–90
12	Daniel 7–8
13	Luke 11–12
14	1 Timothy 1–3
15	Jeremiah 7–8
16	Leviticus 13–16
17	2 Kings 11–15
18	Psalms 91–95
19	Daniel 9–10
20	Luke 13–14
21	1 Timothy 4–6
22	Jeremiah 9–10
23	Leviticus 17–22

24	2 Kings 16–20
25	Psalms 96–100
26	Daniel 11–12
27	Luke 15–16
28	2 Timothy 1–4
29	Jeremiah 11–12
30	Leviticus 23–27
31	2 Kings 21–25

August

1	Psalms 101–105
2	Hosea 1–2
3	Luke 17–18
4	Titus 1–3
5	Jeremiah 13–14
6	Numbers 1–3
7	1 Chronicles 1–5
8	Psalms 106–110
9	Hosea 3–4
10	Luke 19–20
11	Philemon
12	Jeremiah 15–16
13	Numbers 4–6
14	1 Chronicles 6–10
15	Psalms 111–115
16	Hosea 5–7
17	Luke 21–22
18	Hebrews 1–3
19	Jeremiah 17–18
20	Numbers 7–9
21	1 Chronicles 11–15
22	Psalms 116–118; 120
23	Hosea 8–11
24	Luke 23–24
25	Hebrews 4–6
26	Jeremiah 19–20
27	Numbers 10–12
28	1 Chronicles 16–20
29	Psalm 119
30	Hosea 12–14
31	John 1–2

September

1	Hebrews 7–10
2	Jeremiah 21–22
3	Numbers 13–15
4	1 Chronicles 21–24
5	Psalms 121–125

6	Joel 1–3	15	Deuteronomy 1–3	23	Acts 8–10
7	John 3–4	16	2 Chronicles 21–25	24	Revelation 5–8
8	Hebrews 11–13	17	Proverbs 1–5	25	Jeremiah 45–46
9	Jeremiah 23–24	18	Jonah 3–4	26	Deuteronomy 19–21
10	Numbers 16–19	19	John 15–16	27	Nehemiah 1–4
11	1 Chronicles 25–29	20	1 John 1–3	28	Ecclesiastes 1–4
12	Psalms 126–130	21	Jeremiah 35–36	29	Haggai 1–2
13	Amos 1–3	22	Deuteronomy 4–6	30	Acts 11–13
14	John 5–6	23	2 Chronicles 26–30		
15	James 1–3	24	Proverbs 6–10		
16	Jeremiah 25–26	25	Micah 1–3		

December

17	Numbers 20–24	26	John 17–18	1	Revelation 9–11
18	2 Chronicles 1–5	27	1 John 4–5	2	Jeremiah 47–48
19	Psalms 131–135	28	Jeremiah 37–38	3	Deuteronomy 22–24
20	Amos 4–6	29	Deuteronomy 7–9	4	Nehemiah 5–8
21	John 7–8	30	2 Chronicles 31–36	5	Ecclesiastes 5–8
22	James 4–5	31	Proverbs 11–15	6	Zechariah 1–4
23	Jeremiah 27–28			7	Acts 14–16
24	Numbers 25–29			8	Revelation 12–14
25	2 Chronicles 6–10		*November*	9	Jeremiah 49–50
26	Psalms 136–140			10	Deuteronomy 25–27
27	Amos 7–9	1	Micah 4–7	11	Nehemiah 9–13
28	John 9–10	2	John 19–21	12	Ecclesiastes 9–12
29	1 Peter 1–3	3	2 John; 3 John	13	Zechariah 5–9
30	Jeremiah 29–30	4	Jeremiah 39–40	14	Acts 17–20
		5	Deuteronomy 10–12	15	Revelation 15–17
		6	Ezra 1–3	16	Jeremiah 51–52
	October	7	Proverbs 16–20	17	Deuteronomy 28–30
		8	Nahum 1–3	18	Esther 1–5
1	Numbers 30–33	9	Acts 1–3	19	Song of Solomon 1–4
2	2 Chronicles 11–15	10	Jude	20	Zechariah 10–14
3	Psalms 141–145	11	Jeremiah 41–42	21	Acts 21–24
4	Obadiah	12	Deuteronomy 13–15	22	Revelation 18–20
5	John 11–12	13	Ezra 4–7	23	Lamentations 1–2
6	1 Peter 4–5	14	Proverbs 21–25	24	Deuteronomy 31–32
7	Jeremiah 31–32	15	Habakkuk 1–3	25	Esther 6–10
8	Numbers 34–36	16	Acts 4–7	26	Song of Solomon 5–8
9	2 Chronicles 16–20	17	Revelation 1–4	27	Malachi 1–4
10	Psalms 146–150	18	Jeremiah 43–44	28	Acts 25–28
11	Jonah 1–2	19	Deuteronomy 16–18	29	Revelation 21–22
12	John 13–14	20	Ezra 8–10	30	Lamentations 3–5
13	2 Peter 1–3	21	Proverbs 26–31	31	Deuteronomy 33–34
14	Jeremiah 33–34	22	Zephaniah 1–3		

Notes

Chapter 1 God's Calling

1. George O. Wood, "Life's Alternatives," *Pentecostal Evangel* (March 26, 1995): 6.
2. F. B. Meyer, *Joshua* (United Kingdom: Marshall, Morgan, and Scott, 1977), 119.
3. John R. W. Stott, *The Bible Speaks Today: The Message of Ephesians* (Downers Grove, IL: InterVarsity, 1979), 203.
4. Quoted in Os Guinness, *Entrepreneurs of Life,* Trinity Forum Study Series (Colorado Springs: NavPress, 2001), 209–12.

Chapter 2 Illumination

1. *American Bible Society Record* (March 1990), quoting from *McHenry's Quips, Quotes, and Other Notes* (Hendrickson), 236.
2. David Jeremiah, *Turning toward Integrity* (Colorado Springs: Chariot Victor, 1993), 56–57. Used with permission of Cook Communications Ministries. May not be further reproduced. All rights reserved.
3. Warren W. Wiersbe, *Be Faithful* (Colorado Springs: Chariot Victor, 1981), 134–35.
4. Focus on the Family, *The Pastor's Weekly Briefing* (May 2001).
5. Skip Heitzig, *Enjoying Bible Study* (Costa Mesa, CA: Word for Today, 1996), 10–13.

Chapter 3 Power

1. Corrie ten Boom with John and Elizabeth Sherrill, *The Hiding Place* (Chappaqua, NY: Chosen Books, 1971), 185–89. *The Hiding Place* by Corrie ten Boom with John and Elizabeth Sherrill, Chosen Books LLC, Chappaqua, New York. Reprinted with permission of the author.

2. R. Kent Hughes, *Colossians and Philemon: The Supremacy of Christ* (Westchester, IL: Crossway, 1989), 21.

3. James S. Hewitt, ed., *Illustrations Unlimited* (Wheaton: Tyndale, 1988), 419.

4. S. I. McMillan, *None of These Diseases* (Westward, NJ: Revell, 1963), 96.

5. Robert Strand, *Moments for Christmas* (Green Forest, AR: New Leaf Press, 1993), day 2. Reprinted with permission of the publisher.

Chapter 4 Desire

1. David Jeremiah, *Turning toward Joy* (Wheaton: Victor, 1992), 95–96. Used with permission of Cook Communications Ministries. May not be further reproduced. All rights reserved.

2. Os Guinness, *The Call* (Nashville: Word, 1998), 45.

3. David Jeremiah, *Medicine for the Soul*, Turning Point Humor Series (San Diego: Turning Point Ministries tape series, 1997). Used by permission.

4. Jon Courson, *Tree of Life Bible Study: Gospel of Matthew*, vol. 2 (Jacksonville, OR: Tree of Life, 1993), 281.

5. Athletes in Action, *Driving Force*, Heart of a Champion video, (Lebanon, OH: Vision Quest Communication Group, August 2000).

6. *Chariots of Fire*, Allied Stars, Enigma, Ladd Company and Warner Brothers release (1981).

Chapter 5 Faith

1. Robert Strand, *Moments for Graduates* (Green Forest, AR: New Leaf Press, 1993), day 20. Reprinted with permission of the publisher.

2. Warren W. Wiersbe, *Be Rich* (Colorado Springs: Chariot Victor, 1979), 29.

3. Christianity Today International, *Perfect Illustrations for Every Topic and Occasion* (Wheaton: Tyndale, 2002), 260–61. Reprinted with permission of Tyndale House Publishers, Inc.

4. Craig Brian Larson, ed., *Contemporary Illustrations for Preachers, Teachers, and Writers* (Grand Rapids: Baker, 1998), 179.

5. Robert Strand, *Moments for Each Other* (Green Forest, AR: New Leaf Press, 1993), day 2. Reprinted with permission of the publisher.

Chapter 6 Supernatural Intervention

1. Permission obtained from John Plummer, March 24, 2004.
2. See Louis Berkhof, *Systematic Theology* (Grand Rapids: Eerdmans, 1939), 165–78.
3. Calvary Chapel Church, *My God Story* (Fort Lauderdale: Calvary Chapel Church, 2001), 130–32. Copyright 2001. Reprinted with permission of the publisher.
4. John Charles Pollock, *To All the Nations: The Billy Graham Story* (New York: Harper Collins, 1985), chapter 1.
5. Roy L. Laurin, *Romans: Where Life Begins* (Grand Rapids: Kregel, 1948), 321.
6. See Berkhof, *Systematic Theology,* 165–78.
7. Ravi Zacharias, *Deliver Us from Evil: Restoring the Soul in a Disintegrating Culture*, Word audio books on cassette (Dallas: Word, 1996), tape 2, side 2. Zacharias tells the story of his friend Hein Pham (who was his translator in Vietnam). Reprinted with permission of Ravi Zacharias.

Chapter 7 Surrender

1. *God's Little Devotional Book for Men* (Tulsa: Honor Books, 1996), 74–75.
2. Alexander Maclaren, *Expositions of Holy Scripture* (Grand Rapids: Baker, n.d.).
3. John F. MacArthur, *The MacArthur New Testament Commentary: Matthew 8–15* (Chicago: Moody, 1987), 215.

Chapter 8 Courage

1. Gary LaFerla story recounted and rewritten by author, 2003.
2. Hewitt, *Illustrations Unlimited*, 165–66. Reprinted with permission of the publisher.
3. *Our Daily Bread* (June 6, 1992), at www.christianglobe.com/illustrations. *Our Daily Bread* copyright 1992 by RBC Ministries. Reprinted by permission.
4. Guinness, *The Call*, 28–29.
5. Hewitt, *Illustrations Unlimited,* 19–20.

6. A. T. Pierson, *George Mueller of Bristol* (Grand Rapids: Kregel, 1998), 101.

7. *Men of Integrity* 4, no. 5 (September–October 2001); adapted from Don Aycock, *God's Man* (Grand Rapids: Kregel, 1998).

8. Charles R. Swindoll, *Growing Strong in the Seasons of Life* (Portland, OR: Multnomah, 1983), 369. Copyright © 1983 by Charles R. Swindoll, Inc. Used with permission of the Zondervan Corporation.

Chapter 9 Success

1. Strand, *Moments for Graduates,* day 1. Used with permission of the publisher.

2. *San Luis Obispo County Telegram-Tribune*, August 31, 1996, sec. B1.

3. Roy L. Laurin, *Colossians: Where Life Is Established* (Grand Rapids: Kregel, 1948), 142.

4. Donald Grey Barnhouse, *Let Me Illustrate* (Grand Rapids: Baker, 1967), 222.

5. Charles R. Swindoll, *The Finishing Touch* (Dallas: Word, 1994), 622.

6. Source of story unknown.

7. John Phillips, *Exploring the Gospels: John* (Neptune, NJ: Loizeaux Brothers, 1989), 265.

8. Commander Eric J. Berryman, "Strange Things Happen at Sea," *Proceedings* 115.6.1036 (U.S. Naval Institute, June 1989), 48. Reprinted from *Proceedings* with permission; copyright 1989. Reprinted with permission of U.S. Naval Institute www.navalinstitute.org.

9. David Jeremiah; *Turning toward Integrity* (Colorado Springs; ChariotVictor, 1993).

10. Mrs. Charles E. Cowman, *Streams in the Desert*, James G. Reimann updated edition (1925; Grand Rapids: Zondervan, 1997), 158–60. Copyright © 1997 by The Zondervan Coproration. Used with permission of the Zondervan Corporation.

Gary LaFerla is a seasoned and dynamic speaker who for more than twenty years has had experience in professional marketing, conference speaking, crusade management, and broadcasting in both the domestic and international arenas. He has filled such roles as vice president of marketing and director of national sales for the corporate sector and chairman of the board, CEO, senior pastor, and director of crusade management with the nonprofit sector.

As founder of G3 International, a new organization dedicated to global evangelism, he directs and speaks at international crusades that also include leadership development, broadcasting, and humanitarian aid. Gary is the senior pastor of Calvary Chapel in Akron, Ohio.

Gary is touring the United States, speaking at churches as well as conducting "Finding Your Way" conferences on the subject of finding God's will in our lives. Having traveled widely, Gary enjoys interacting with people and helping them maximize their lives for Christ.

He earned a B.A. in International Business Administration from California State University at Fullerton, California, and has done graduate work in apologetics and expository preaching at Simon Greenleaf School of Law and Azusa Pacific University.

Gary and his wife, Debbie, have been married for sixteen years. They have two children, Chelsea (age thirteen) and Christopher (age nine).

To book Gary LaFerla for a speaking engagement or to bring a "Finding Your Way" conference to your area, please call (330) 848-2000 or contact us by email on the web at www .G3international.org.